T0155670

Java Image Processing Recipes

With OpenCV and JVM

Nicolas Modrzyk

Apress®

Java Image Processing Recipes

Nicolas Modrzyk
Tokyo, Japan

ISBN-13 (pbk): 978-1-4842-3464-8   ISBN-13 (electronic): 978-1-4842-3465-5
https://doi.org/10.1007/978-1-4842-3465-5

Library of Congress Control Number: 2018936912

Managing Director, Apress Media LLC: Welmoed Spahr
Acquisitions Editor: Susan McDermott / Shiva Ramachandran
Development Editor: Laura Berendson
Coordinating Editor: Rita Fernando

Cover designed by eStudioCalamar

Cover image designed by Freepik (www.freepik.com)

Distributed to the book trade worldwide by Springer Science+Business Media New York, 233 Spring Street, 6th Floor, New York, NY 10013. Phone 1-800-SPRINGER, fax (201) 348-4505, e-mail orders-ny@springer-sbm.com, or visit www.springeronline.com. Apress Media, LLC is a California LLC and the sole member (owner) is Springer Science + Business Media Finance Inc (SSBM Finance Inc). SSBM Finance Inc is a **Delaware** corporation.

For information on translations, please e-mail rights@apress.com, or visit http://www.apress.com/rights-permissions.

Apress titles may be purchased in bulk for academic, corporate, or promotional use. eBook versions and licenses are also available for most titles. For more information, reference our Print and eBook Bulk Sales web page at http://www.apress.com/bulk-sales.

Any source code or other supplementary material referenced by the author in this book is available to readers on GitHub via the book's product page, located at www.apress.com/9781484234648. For more detailed information, please visit http://www.apress.com/source-code.

Printed on acid-free paper

Table of Contents

TABLE OF CONTENTS

About the Author

 **Nicolas Modrzyk** is currently Chief Technical Officer of Karabiner Software and a leader of development teams.

He is also an active contributor to the open source software community. As a developer and technical consultant, Nico has been involved over many years in designing large-scale server applications for a video conferencing company, managing enormous clusters of databases through high-performance middleware developed from scratch, enabling Japanese leaders with content management and process management systems, and pushing the boundaries of business processes for leading Asian companies.

Nico is an ardent advocate of Agile methods and is focused on getting the job done right to satisfy clients. He also loves to push friends and team members to challenge themselves and reach their goals. He has lived by those empowering standards in various countries, including France, America, Ireland, Japan, China, and India. Nico is also the author of a few other books on the Clojure programming language, in both English and Japanese.

He is currently based in Tokyo, Japan, where he is often found after hours playing soccer, hiking, performing live concerts with his guitar, and enjoying life with friends and colleagues.

About the Technical Reviewer

Aakash Kag is an AI developer at Manacola Private Ltd. He has two years of experience in big data analytics. He is a postgraduate in Computer Science with a specialization in Big Data Analytics. Aakash has also made contributions to the Microsoft bot builder.

Currently, Aakash is working on problems related to Conversational Bots and Natural Language Understanding.

He is passionate about Machine Learning meetups, where he often presents talks.

Acknowledgments

It's been the most amazing typing race of my life to get this book out on time, and to beat time and the odds, I got support from so many people that it would take another book just to write the list of names. So ...

Thank you to all my family, brother, sister, friends, Abe-san, all my soccer friends, people still having Guinness pints in Ireland (keep one for me!), the awesome people in America (who sometimes send LP records... when I need them the most), Sawada-san, Chris and the Biners, my French friends (always there for support even when not being asked for it), publisher Apress, Divya for never being impressed and kicking my butt on a regular basis, and ... the people deep in my heart for your NEVER-ENDING support. I never could have finished this without you. I appreciate it so much.

And, of course... thank you to my two beautiful daughters, Mei and Manon, for keeping up and always doing their best even during hard times. You simply rock! I love you.

Introduction

My father is a dentist. When I was in my early childhood, he used to repeat the same sentence over and over again, which as far as I can remember and translate properly now was something like:

"Son, get the right tool for the job."

And as he was looking at me trying to wash the car with the wrong washing product and spending twice the amount of time that I should have, I knew somewhere deep inside of me that he was right.

He did not use a screwdriver to pull out teeth from his patients, and he had what seemed like twenty different brushes to clean each type of tooth. I even thought it was funny at the time.

Fast-forward thirty years later; I was talking about this book with him and he added:

"Well, son, you know, it's not only about the right tool, it's about the right tool at the right time."

And so, this is the philosophy guiding this book.

OpenCV, the computer vision library, has always been one of the tools to work on imaging- and vision-related projects, even more so with every improvement in AI and neural networks. But OpenCV was always taking some time to get the right libraries, and the right build tools, and the right build settings, and so forth.

The vision of the Clojure wrapper Origami is to bring you all the power of OpenCV to your hands almost instantly, along with a pleasurable syntax. This way we hope you can focus and spend your time entirely on the job, not on the tool.

Chapter 1 will introduce you to pure OpenCV on the JVM using Java, Scala, and Kotlin and present some of their shortcomings.

Chapter 2 will present Origami, the Clojure wrapper, and how to use it to perform simple image manipulation.

Chapter 3 will get you up to speed with more advanced concepts of image manipulation, like shape finding, but still in a pleasant syntax.

Finally, Chapter 4 moves to video analysis, with shape finding, transformations, and various techniques to analyze real-time streams with ease.

CHAPTER 1

OpenCV
on the JavaVM

A few years ago, while on a trip to Shanghai, a very good friend of mine bought me a massive book on OpenCV. It had tons of photography manipulation, real-time video analysis samples, and in-depth explanations that were very appealing, and I just could not wait to get things up and running on my local environment.

OpenCV, as you may know, stands for Open Source Computer Vision; it is an open source library that gives you ready-to-use implementations of advanced imaging algorithms, going from simple-to-use but advanced image manipulations to shape recognition and real-time video analysis spy powers.

The very core of OpenCV is a multidimensional matrix object named Mat. Mat is going to be our best friend all along this book. Input objects are Mat, operations are run on Mat, and the output of our work is also going to be Mat.

Mat, even though it is going to be our best friend, is a C++ object, and as such, is not the easiest of friends to bring and show around. You have to recompile, install, and be very gentle about the new environment almost anywhere you take him.

But Mat can be packaged.

Mat, even though he is a native (i.e., runs natively), can be dressed to run on the Java Virtual Machine almost without anyone noticing.

© Nicolas Modrzyk 2018
N. Modrzyk, *Java Image Processing Recipes*, https://doi.org/10.1007/978-1-4842-3465-5_1

This first chapter wants to get you introduced to work with OpenCV with some of the main languages of the Java Virtual Machine, namely Java of course, but also the easier-to-read Scala and the Google-hyped Kotlin.

To run all these different languages in a similar fashion, you will first get (re-?)introduced to a Java build tool named leiningen and then you will move on to use simple OpenCV functions with it.

The road of this first chapter will take you to the door of the similarly JVM-based language Clojure, which will give your OpenCV code instant visual feedback for great creativity. That will be for Chapter 2.

1-1 Getting Started with Leiningen
Problem

You remember the write-once-run-everywhere quote, and you would like to compile Java code and run the Java program in an easy and portable manner across different machines. Obviously, you can always revert to using the plain javac command to compile Java code, and pure Java on the command line to run your compiled code, but we are in the 21st century, and hey, you are looking for something more.

Whatever the programming language, setting up your working environment by hand is quite a task, and when you are done, it is hard to share with other people.

Using a build tool, you can define in simple ways what is required to work on your project, and get other users to get started quickly.

You would like to get started with an easy-to-work-with build tool.

Solution

Leiningen is a build tool targeting (mostly) the JavaVM. It is similar in that sense to other famous ones like (Remember? The) Ant, (Oh My God) Maven, and (it used to work) Gradle.

Once the leiningen command is installed, you can use it to create new JavaVM projects based on templates, and run them without the usual headaches.

This recipe shows how to install Leiningen quickly and run your first Java program with it.

How it works

You will start by simply installing Leiningen where you need it, and then creating a blank Java project with it.

Note   Installing Leiningen requires Java 8 to be installed on your machine. Note also that due to the fact that Java 9 is solving old problems by breaking current solutions, we will choose to keep Java 8 for now.

Installing Leiningen

The Leiningen web site itself is hosted and can be found at

```
https://leiningen.org/
```

At the top of the Leiningen page, you can find the four easy steps to install the tool manually yourself.

So here it goes, on macOS and Unix:

1. Download the lein script

    - ```
      https://raw.githubusercontent.com/
      technomancy/leiningen/stable/bin/lein
      ```

2. Place it on your $PATH where your shell can find it
    (e.g., ~/bin)
      ```

3. Set it to be executable (chmod a+x ~/bin/lein)

4. Run it from a terminal, lein, and it will download the self-install package

And on Windows:

1. Download the lein.bat batch script

   - `https://raw.githubusercontent.com/technomancy/leiningen/stable/bin/lein.bat`

2. Place it on your C:/Windows/System32 folder, using admin permission

3. Open a command prompt and run it, lein, and it will download the self-install package

---

On Unix, you can almost always use a package manager. Brew, on macOS, has a package for leiningen.

On Windows, there is also a good Windows installer, located at `https://djpowell.github.io/leiningen-win-installer/`.

If you are a Chocolatey fan, Windows has a package for Chocolatey as well: `https://chocolatey.org/packages/Lein`.

If you finished the install process successfully on a terminal or command prompt, you should be able to check the version of the installed tool. On the first run, Leiningen downloads its own internal dependencies, but any other subsequent runs will regularly be fast.

```
NikoMacBook% lein -v
Leiningen 2.7.1 on Java 1.8.0_144 Java HotSpot(TM) 64-Bit
Server VM
```

Creating a New OpenCV-Ready Java Project with Leiningen

Leiningen mainly works around a text file, named **project.clj,** where the metadata, dependencies, plug-ins, and settings for those projects are defined in a simple map.

When you execute commands on the project calling the lein command, lein will look into that project.clj to find the relevant information it needs regarding that project.

Leiningen comes with ready-to-use project templates, but in order to understand them properly, let's first walk through a first example step by step.

For a leiningen Java project, you need two files:

- One that describes the project, project.clj

- One file with some Java code in it, here Hello.java

A first project simple directory structure looks like this:

```
.
├── java
│   └── Hello.java
└── project.clj

1 directory, 2 files
```

For peace of mind, we will keep the code of this first Java example pretty simple.

```
public class Hello {
    public static void main(String[] args) {
            System.out.println("beginning of a journey");
    }
}
```

5

Now let's see the content of the text file named project.clj in a bit of detail:

```
(defproject hellojava "0.1"
  :java-source-paths ["java"]
  :dependencies [[org.clojure/clojure "1.8.0"]]
  :main Hello)
```

This is actually Clojure code, but let's simply think of it as a domain specific language (DSL), a language to describe a project in simple terms.

For convenience, each term is described in Table 1-1.

Table 1-1. *Leiningen Project Metadata*

Word	Usage
Defproject	Entry point to define a project
Hellojava	The name of the project
0.1	A string describing the version
:java-source-paths	A list of directories relative to the project folder, where you will put Java code files
:dependencies	The list of external libraries and their versions needed to run the project
[[org.clojure/clojure "1.8.0"]]	By default, the list contains Clojure, which is needed to run leiningen. You will put OpenCV libraries here later on
:main	The name of the Java class that will be executed by default

Now go ahead and create the preceding directory and file structure, and copy-paste the content of each file accordingly.

Once done, run your first leiningen command:

```
lein run
```

6

The command will generate the following output on your terminal or console depending on your environment.

```
Compiling 1 source files to /Users/niko/hellojava/target/classes
beginning of a journey
```

Whoo-hoo! The journey has begun! But, wait, what happened just there?

A bit of magic was involved. The leiningen run command will make Leiningen execute a compiled Java class main method. The class to be executed was defined in the project's metadata, and as you remember, that would be **Hello**.

Before executing the Java compiled class there is a need to... compile it. By default, Leiningen does compilation before performing the run command, and so this is where the "Compiling ..." message came out from.

Along the way, you may have noticed that a target folder was created inside your project folder, with a classes folder, and a Hello.class file inside.

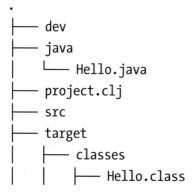

```
.
├── dev
├── java
│   └── Hello.java
├── project.clj
├── src
├── target
│   ├── classes
│   │   ├── Hello.class
```

The target/classes folder is where the compiled Java bytecode goes by default, and that same target folder is then added to the Java execution runtime (classpath).

The execute phase triggered by "lein run" follows, and the code block from the main method of the Hello class is executed; then the message prints out.

```
beginning of a journey.
```

You may ask: "What if I have multiple Java files, and want to run a different one than the main one?"

This is a very valid question, as you will be probably doing that a few times in this first chapter to write and run the different code samples.

Say you write a second Java class in a file named Hello2.java in the same Java folder, along with some updated journey content.

```java
import static java.lang.System.out;
public class Hello2 {
    public static void main(String[] args) {
        String[] text = new String[]{
                "Sometimes it's the journey that ",
                "teaches you a lot about your destination.",
                "--",
                "- Drake"};
        for(String t : text) out.println(t);
    }
}
```

To run that exact main method from the Hello2.java file, you would call lein run with the optional –m option, where m stands for main, and then the name of the main Java class to use.

```
lein run -m Hello2
```

This gives you the following output:

```
Compiling 1 source files to /Users/niko/hellojava/target/
classes
Sometimes it's the journey that
teaches you a lot about your destination.
--
- Drake
```

Great. With those instructions, you now know enough to go ahead and run your first OpenCV Java program.

1-2 Writing Your First OpenCV Java Program

Problem

You would like to use Leiningen to have a Java project setup where you can use OpenCV libraries directly.

You would like to run Java code making use of OpenCV, but you got headaches already (while compiling the opencv wrapper yourself), so you would like to make this step as simple as possible.

Solution

Recipe 1-1 presented Leiningen to help you with all the basic required setup. From there, you can add a dependency on the OpenCV C++ library and its Java wrapper.

How it works

For this first OpenCV example, we will get set up with a Leiningen project template, where the project.clj file and the project folders are already defined for you. Leiningen project templates do not have to be

9

downloaded separately and can be called upon to create new projects using Leiningen's integrated new command.

To create this project on your local machine, on the command line, let's call the command of lein.

Whether on Windows or Mac, the command gives

```
lein new jvm-opencv hellocv
```

What the preceding command basically does is

1. create a new project folder named hellocv

2. create directories and files with the content of the folder based on a template named jvm-opencv

After running the command, the rather simple following project files are created:

```
.
├── java
│   └── HelloCv.java
└── project.clj
```

That does not seem too impressive, but actually those are almost the same as the two files from the previous recipe: a project descriptor and a Java file.

The **project.clj** content is a slightly modified version from before:

```
(defproject hellocv "0.1.0-SNAPSHOT"
  :java-source-paths ["java"]
  :main HelloCv
  :repositories [
  ["vendredi" "http://hellonico.info:8081/repository/
hellonico/"]]
  :dependencies [[org.clojure/clojure "1.8.0"]
                 [opencv/opencv "3.3.1"]
                 [opencv/opencv-native "3.3.1"]])
```

You probably have noticed straightaway three new lines you have not seen before.

First of all is the `repositories` section, which indicates a new repository location to find dependencies. The one provided here is the author's public repository where custom builds of opencv (and others) can be found.

The opencv core dependency and the native dependency have been compiled and uploaded on that public repository and provided for your convenience.

The two dependencies are as follows:

- opencv

- opencv-native

Why two dependencies, you might ask?

Well one of these dependencies is the opencv code in c++ for macOS, Windows, or Linux. The opencv core is the platform-independent Java wrapper that calls the platform-dependent c++ code.

This is actually the way the opencv code is delivered when you do the compilation of OpenCV yourself.

For convenience, the packaged opencv-native dependency contains the native code for Windows, Linux, and macOS.

The Java code in file HelloCv.java, located in the Java folder, is a simple helloworld kind of example, which will simply load OpenCV native libraries; its content is shown in the following.

```
import org.opencv.core.Core;
import org.opencv.core.CvType;
import org.opencv.core.Mat;
```

```
public class HelloCv {
    public static void main(String[] args) throws Exception {
        System.loadLibrary(Core.NATIVE_LIBRARY_NAME); // ①
        Mat hello = Mat.eye(3,3, CvType.CV_8UC1); // ②
        System.out.println(hello.dump());   // ③
    }
}
```

What does the code do?

- ① It tells the Java runtime to load the native opencv library via loadLibrary. This is a required step when working with OpenCV and needs to be done once in the lifetime of your application.

- ② A native Mat object can then be created via a Java object.

- Mat is basically an image container, like a matrix, and here we tell it to be of size 3×3: height of three pixels, width of three pixels, where each pixel is of type 8UC1, a weird name that simply means one channel (C1) of eight bits (unsigned) integer (8U).

- ③ Finally, it prints the content of the mat (matrix) object.

The project is ready to be run as you have done before, and whichever platform you are running on, the same leiningen run command will do the job:

```
NikoMacBook% lein run
```

The command output is shown in the following.

```
Retrieving opencv/opencv-native/3.3.1/opencv-native-3.3.1.jar
from vendredi
Compiling 1 source files to /Users/niko/hellocv2/target/classes
```

```
[  1,    0,    0;
   0,    1,    0;
   0,    0,    1]
```

The 1s and 0s you see printed are the actual content of the matrix that was created.

1-3 Automatically Compiling and Running Code

Problem

While the lein command is pretty versatile, you would like to start the process in the background and get the code to be automatically run for you as you change the code.

Solution

Leiningen comes with an auto plug-in. Once enabled, that plug-in watches changes in patterns of files and triggers a command. Let's use it!

How it works

When you create a project using the jvm-opencv template (see Recipe 1-2), you will notice that the content of the file project.clj is slightly longer than presented in the recipe. It was actually more like this:

```
(defproject hellocv3 "0.1.0-SNAPSHOT"
  :java-source-paths ["java"]
  :main HelloCv
  :repositories [
```

```
["vendredi" "http://hellonico.info:8081/repository/
hellonico/"]]
:plugins [[lein-auto "0.1.3"]]
:auto {:default {:file-pattern #"\.(java)$"}}
:dependencies [[org.clojure/clojure "1.8.0"]
               [opencv/opencv "3.3.1"]
               [opencv/opencv-native "3.3.1"]]])
```

Two extra lines have been highlighted. One line is the addition of the lein-auto plug-in in a :plugins section of the project metadata.

The second line, the :auto section, defines the file pattern to watch for changes; here, files that end in Java will activate the refresh of the auto subcommand.

Let's go back to the command line, where now we will be prepending the auto command before the usual run command. The command you need to write is now as follows:

```
lein auto run
```

The first time you run it, it will give the same output as the previous recipe, but with some added extra lines:

```
auto> Files changed: java/HelloCv.java
auto> Running: lein run
Compiling 1 source files to /Users/niko/hellocv3/target/classes
[  1,   0,   0;
   0,   1,   0;
   0,   0,   1]
auto> Completed.
```

Nice; note here that the leiningen command has not finished running and is actually listening for file changes.

From there, go ahead and update the Java code of HelloCv, with a `Mat` object of a different size. So replace the following line:

```
Mat hello = Mat.eye(3,3, CvType.CV_8UC1);
```

with

```
Mat hello = Mat.eye(5,5, CvType.CV_8UC1);
```

The updated code says that the Mat object is now a 5×5 matrix, each pixel still being represented by a one-byte integer.

And look at the terminal or console where the leiningen command was running to see the output being updated:

```
auto> Files changed: java/HelloCv.java
auto> Running: lein run
Compiling 1 source files to /Users/niko/hellocv3/target/classes
[  1,   0,   0,   0,   0;
   0,   1,   0,   0,   0;
   0,   0,   1,   0,   0;
   0,   0,   0,   1,   0;
   0,   0,   0,   0,   1]
auto> Completed.
```

Note how this time the printed matrix of the mat object is made of five rows of five columns.

1-4 Using a Better Text Editor
Problem

You may have used your own text editor to type in code up to now, but you would like a slightly better working environment for working with OpenCV.

Solution

While this is not a final solution and other different environments may be more productive for you, I found using a simple setup based on Github's Atom editor to be quite effective. That editor will be of great use as well when typing code in real time.

One of the main reasons to enjoy working in Atom is that pictures are reloaded on the fly, so that when working on an image, updates to that image will be automatically reflected directly on your screen. As far as I know, this is the only editor with such a support. Let's see how it works!

How it works

Installing the base Atom editor should be a simple matter of going to the web site and downloading the software, so simply go ahead and download the installer.

```
https://atom.io/
```

Not only is atom a good editor by default, but it is easy to add plug-ins to match your work style.

Here for OpenCV, we would like to add three plug-ins:

- one generic IDE plug-in

- one plug-in for the Java language, making use of the

- last one for a terminal inside the editor.

The three plug-ins are shown in Figures 1-1, 1-2, and 1-3.

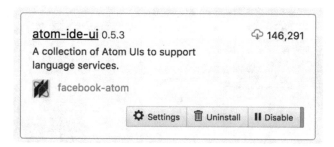

Figure 1-1. *Atom ide-ui plug-in*

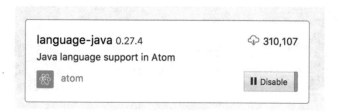

Figure 1-2. *Atom Java language plug-in*

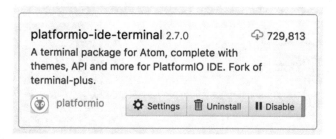

Figure 1-3. *Atom ide-terminal plug-in*

The terminal that opens at the bottom will let you type the same "lein auto run" command, so you do not need a separate command prompt or terminal window for the autorunning feature of Leiningen. That keeps all your code writing in a single window.

Ideally, your Atom layout would look something like either Figure 1-4 or Figure 1-5.

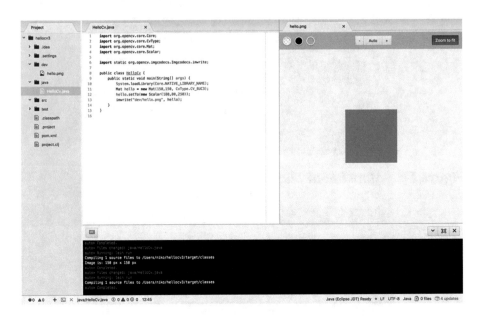

Figure 1-4. *Atom IDE standard layout*

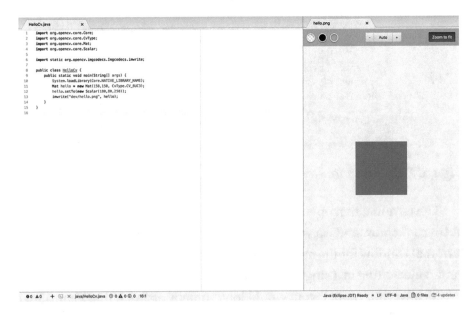

Figure 1-5. *Atom IDE clean layout*

Note that autocompletion for Java is now enabled through Atom's Java plug-in too, so typing function names will show a drop-down menu of available options, as shown in Figure 1-6:

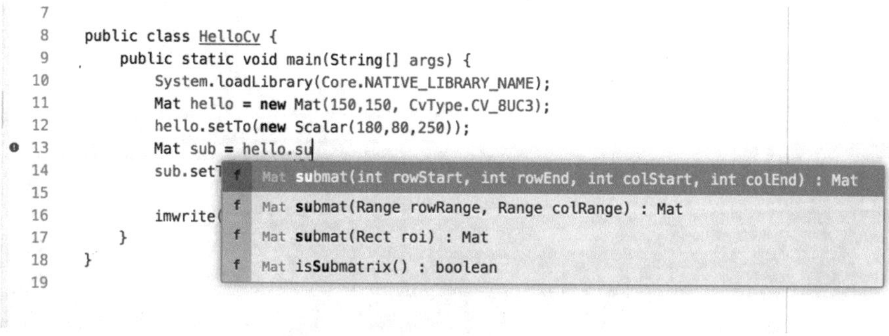

```
 7
 8    public class HelloCv {
 9        public static void main(String[] args) {
10            System.loadLibrary(Core.NATIVE_LIBRARY_NAME);
11            Mat hello = new Mat(150,150, CvType.CV_8UC3);
12            hello.setTo(new Scalar(180,80,250));
13            Mat sub = hello.su
14            sub.setT  f  Mat submat(int rowStart, int rowEnd, int colStart, int colEnd) : Mat
15
16            imwrite(   f  Mat submat(Range rowRange, Range colRange) : Mat
17        }          f  Mat submat(Rect roi) : Mat
18    }
19                   f  Mat isSubmatrix() : boolean
```

Figure 1-6. *Atom IDE autocompletion*

Finally, updates on the image, while not able to be seen in real time, can be seen while saving the file, and if you open that file in the background it will be refreshed on each save, a save being done with OpenCV's function `imwrite`.

So, with the `leiningen auto run` command running in the background, when the Java file is saved, the compilation/run cycle is triggered and the image is updated.

Figure 1-7 shows how the picture onscreen is visually updated, even without a single user action (apart from file save).

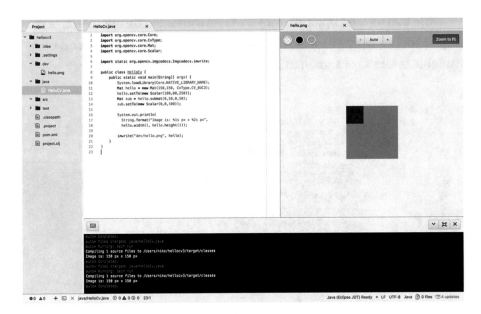

Figure 1-7. *Automatically updated image on Java file save*

You will see that later in this chapter, but for reference right now, here is the code snippet changing the color of one subsection of the Mat object using the submat function.

```
import org.opencv.core.Core;
import org.opencv.core.CvType;
import org.opencv.core.Mat;
import org.opencv.core.Scalar;

import static org.opencv.imgcodecs.Imgcodecs.imwrite;

public class HelloCv {
    public static void main(String[] args) {
        System.loadLibrary(Core.NATIVE_LIBRARY_NAME);
        Mat hello = new Mat(150,150, CvType.CV_8UC3);
        hello.setTo(new Scalar(180,80,250));
        Mat sub = hello.submat(0,50,0,50);
```

```
        sub.setTo(new Scalar(0,0,100));
        imwrite("dev/hello.png", hello);
    }
}
```

You now have a setup to enjoy full-blown OpenCV powers. Let's use them.

1-5 Learning the Basics of the OpenCV Mat Object

Problem

You would live to get a better grasp of the OpenCV object Mat, since it is at the core of the OpenCV framework.

Solution

Let's review how to create mat objects and inspect their content through a few core samples.

How it works

This recipe needs the same setup that was completed in the previous recipe.

To create a very simple matrix with only one channel per "dot," you would usually use one of the following three static functions from the Mat class: zeros, eye, ones.

It easier to see what each of those does by looking at each output in Table 1-2.

Table 1-2. *Static Functions to Create One Channel per Pixel Mat*

Function Name	Code	Usage	Output
zeros	Mat.zeros(3,3,CV_8UC1)	When you want the new mat to be all zeros	[0, 0, 0; 0, 0, 0; 0, 0, 0]
eye	Mat.eye(3, 3, CV_8UC1)	When you want all zeros except when x=y	[1, 0, 0; 0, 1, 0; 0, 0, 1]
ones	Mat.ones(3,3,CV_8UC1)	When you want all ones	[1, 1, 1; 1, 1, 1; 1, 1, 1]
(any of the preceding)	Mat.ones(1,1,CV_8UC3)	Each pixel is of 3 channels	[1, 0, 0]

If you have used OpenCV before (and if you haven't yet, please trust us), you will remember that **CV_8UC1** is the OpenCV slang word for eight bits unsigned per channel, and one channel per pixel, so a matrix of 3×3 will therefore have nine values.

Its cousin **CV_8UC3**, as you would have guessed, assigns three channels per pixel, and thus a 1×1 Mat object would have three values. You would usually use this type of Mat when working with Red, Blue, Green, or RGB, images. It also is the default format when loading images.

This first example simply shows three ways of loading a one-channel-per-pixel Mat object and one way to load a three-channels-per-pixel Mat object.

```
import org.opencv.core.Core;
import org.opencv.core.Mat;
import static java.lang.System.loadLibrary;
import static java.lang.System.out;
```

```java
import static org.opencv.core.CvType.CV_8UC1;
import static org.opencv.core.CvType.CV_8UC3;

public class SimpleOpenCV {
    static {
            loadLibrary(Core.NATIVE_LIBRARY_NAME);
    }

    public static void main(String[] args) {
        Mat mat = Mat.eye(3, 3, CV_8UC1);
        out.println("mat = ");
        out.println(mat.dump());

        Mat mat2 = Mat.zeros(3,3,CV_8UC1);
        out.println("mat2 = ");
        out.println(mat2.dump());

        Mat mat3 = Mat.ones(3,3,CV_8UC1);
        out.println("mat3 = " );
        out.println(mat3.dump());

        Mat mat4 = Mat.zeros(1,1,CV_8UC3);
        out.println("mat4 = " );
        out.println(mat4.dump());
    }
}
```

The last Mat object, mat4, is the one containing three channels per pixel. As you can see when you try to dump the object, a three-zeros array is created.

CV_8UC1 and **CV_8UC3** are the two most common types of format per pixel, but many others exist and are defined in the **CvType** class.

When doing mat-to-mat computations, you may eventually also need to use float values per channel. Here is how to achieve that:

```
Mat mat5 = Mat.ones(3,3,CvType.CV_64FC3);
out.println("mat5 = " );
out.println(mat5.dump());
```

And the output matrix:

```
mat5 =
[1, 0, 0, 1, 0, 0, 1, 0, 0;
 1, 0, 0, 1, 0, 0, 1, 0, 0;
 1, 0, 0, 1, 0, 0, 1, 0, 0]
```

In many situations, you would probably not create the matrix from scratch yourself, but simply load the image from a file.

1-6 Loading Images from a File

Problem

You would like to load an image file to convert it to a Mat object for digital manipulation.

Solution

OpenCV has a simple function to read an image from a file, named imread. It usually takes only a file path on the local file system to the image, but it may also have a type parameter. Let's see how to use the different forms of imread.

How it works

The imread function is located in the Imgcodecs class of the same named package.

Its standard usage is down to simply giving the path of the file. Supposing you have downloaded an image of kittens from a Google search and stored it in **images/kittenjpg** (Figure 1-8), the code gives the following:

```
Mat mat = Imgcodecs.imread("images/kitten.jpg");
out.println("mat ="+mat.width()+" x "+mat.height()+","+mat.
type());
```

Figure 1-8. *Running kitten*

If the kitten image is found and loaded properly, the following message will be shown on the output of the console:

```
mat =350 x 234,16
```

Note that if the file is not found, no exception is thrown, and no error message is reported, but the loaded Mat object will be empty, so no row and no column:

```
mat =0 x 0,0
```

Depending on how you code, you may feel the need to wrap the loading code with a size check to make sure that the file was found and the image decoded properly.

It is also possible to load the picture in black-and-white mode (Figure 1-9). This is done by passing another parameter to the imread function.

```
Mat mat = Imgcodecs.imread(
    "images/kitten.jpg",
    Imgcodecs.IMREAD_GRAYSCALE);
```

Figure 1-9. *Grayscale loading*

That other parameter is taken from the same Imgcodecs class.

Here, IMREAD_GRAYSCALE forces the reencoding of the image on load, and turns the Mat object into grayscale mode.

Other options can be passed to the imread function for some specific handling of channels and depth of the image; the most useful of them are described in Table 1-3.

Table 1-3. *Image Reading Options*

Parameter	Effect
IMREAD_REDUCED_GRAYSCALE_2 IMREAD_REDUCED_COLOR_2 IMREAD_REDUCED_GRAYSCALE_4 IMREAD_REDUCED_COLOR_4 IMREAD_REDUCED_GRAYSCALE_8 IMREAD_REDUCED_COLOR_8	Reduce the size of the image on load by a factor of 2, 4, or 8. This means dividing the width and the height by that number. At the same time, specify the color or grayscale mode. Grayscale means one-channel grayscale mode. Color means three-channel RGB.
IMREAD_LOAD_GDAL	Use the GDAL driver to load raster format images.
IMREAD_GRAYSCALE	Load the picture in one-channel grayscale mode.
IMREAD_IGNORE_ORIENTATION	If set, do not rotate the image according to EXIF's orientation flag.

Figure 1-10 shows what happens when the image is loaded in REDUCED_COLOR_8.

Figure 1-10. *Reduced size loading*

As you may have noticed, no indication of the image format was needed when loading the image with imread. OpenCV does all the image decoding, depending on a combination of the file extension and binary data found in the file.

1-7 Saving Images into a File
Problem

You want to be able to save an image using OpenCV.

Solution

OpenCV has a sibling function to imread used to write files, named imwrite, similarly hosted by the class Imgcodecs. It usually takes only a file path on the local file system pointing where to store the image, but it can also take some parameters to modify the way the image is stored.

How it works

The function imwrite works similarly to imread, except of course it also needs the Mat object to store, along with the path.

The first code snippet simply saves the cat image that was loaded in color:

```
Mat mat = imread("images/glasses.jpg");
imwrite("target/output.jpg", mat);
```

Figure 1-11 shows the content of output.jpg picture.

Figure 1-11. *JPEG formatted image on disk*

Now, you can also change the format while saving the Mat object simply by specifying a different extension. For example, to save in Portable Network Graphic (PNG) format, just specify a different extension when calling imwrite.

```
Mat mat = imread("images/glasses.jpg");
imwrite("target/output.png", mat);
```

Without working with encoding and crazy byte manipulation, your output file is indeed saved in PNG format.

You can give saving parameters to imwrite, the most needed ones being compression parameters.

For example, as per the official documentation:

- For JPEG, you can use the parameter CV_IMWRITE_ JPEG_QUALITY, which value is in the range 0 to 100 (the higher the better). The default value is 95.

- For PNG, it can be the compression level () from 0 to 9. A higher value means a smaller size and longer compression time. The default value is 3.

Compressing the output file by using a compression parameter is done through another opencv object named MatOfInt, which is a matrix of integers, or in simpler terms, an array.

```
MatOfInt moi = new MatOfInt(CV_IMWRITE_PNG_COMPRESSION, 9);
Imgcodecs.imwrite("target/output.png", mat, moi);
```

This will enable compression on the png. And by checking the filesize you can actually see that the png file is at least 10% smaller.

1-8 Cropping a Picture with Submat

Problem

You would like to save only a given subsection of an image.

Solution

The main focus of this short recipe is to introduce the submat function. Submat gives you back a Mat object that is a submatrix or subsection of the original.

How it works

We will take a cat picture and extract only the part we want with submat. The cat picture used for this example is shown in Figure 1-12.

Figure 1-12. *A cat*

Of course, you can use whichever cat picture you like. Let's start by reading the file normally, with imread.

```
Mat mat = Imgcodecs.imread("images/cat.jpg");
out.println(mat);
```

As you may notice, **println** gives you some info about the Mat object itself. Most of it is informative memory addressing, so you can hack the memory directly, but it also shows whether the Mat object is a submat or not. In this case, since this is the original picture, it is set to false.

```
[ 1200*1600*CV_8UC3,
  isCont=true,
  isSubmat=false,
  nativeObj=0x7fa7da5b0a50,
dataAddr=0x122c63000 ]
```

Autocompletion in the Atom editor presents you the different versions of the submat function as shown in Figure 1-13.

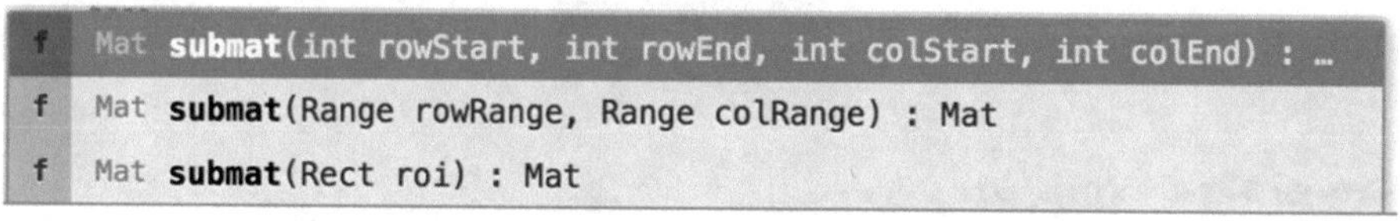

Figure 1-13. *Submat with different parameters*

Now let's use the submat function in its first form, where submat takes start and end parameters, one for each row and column:

```
Mat submat = mat.submat(250,650,600,1000);
out.println(submat);
```

Printing the object shows that the newly created Mat object is indeed a submat.

```
Mat [ 400*400*CV_8UC3,
isCont=false,
isSubmat=true,
nativeObj=0x7fa7da51e730,
dataAddr=0x122d88688 ]
```

You can act directly on the submat just like a regular Mat, so you could start for example by saving it.

```
Imgcodecs.imwrite("output/subcat.png", submat);
```

With the range nicely adapted to the original cat picture, the output of the saved image is shown in Figure 1-14:

Figure 1-14. *Sub-cat*

The nice thing is that not only can you act on the submat, but it also reflects on the original Mat object as well. So if you apply a blur effect to the cat's face on the submat and save the whole mat (not the submat), only the cat's face will look blurry. See how that works:

```
Imgproc.blur(submat,submat, new Size(25.0, 25.0));
out.println(submat);
Imgcodecs.imwrite("output/blurcat.png", mat);
```

blur is a key function of class **org.opencv.imgproc.Imgproc**. It takes a size object as a parameter, to specify the surface to consider per pixel when applying the blur effect, and so the bigger the size, the stronger the blur effect.

See the result in Figure 1-15, where if you look carefully, only the face of the cat is actually blurred, **and** this is the exact face we saved earlier on.

Figure 1-15. *Poor blurred cat*

As you have seen in the contextual helper menu for the submat function, there are two other ways to grab the submat.

One way is with two ranges, the first one for a range of rows (y, or height), and the second ones for a range of columns (x, or width), both created using the Range class.

```
Mat submat2 = mat.submat(new Range(250,650), new Range(600,1000));
```

Another way is with a rectangle, where you give top left coordinates first, then the size of the rectangle.

```
Mat submat3 = mat.submat(new Rect(600, 250, 400, 400));
```

This last way of using submat is one of the most used since it is the most natural. Also, when finding objects within a picture, you can use the bounding box of that object, which type is a Rect object.

Note that, as you have seen, changing a submat has collateral damage effects on the underlying Mat. So if you decide to set the color of a submat to blue:

```
submat3.setTo(new Scalar(255,0,0));
```

```
Imgcodecs.imwrite("output/submat3_2.png", submat3);
Imgcodecs.imwrite("output/submat3_3.png", submat2);
Imgcodecs.imwrite("output/submat3_4.png", mat);
```

Then Figure 1-16 shows the blue cat face of **both** submat3_2.png and submat3_3.png.

Figure 1-16. *Blue cat face*

But those changes to the submat also update the underlying mat, as shown in Figure 1-17!!

Figure 1-17. *Blue cat face in big picture*

So the idea here is to be careful where and when using submat, but most of the time this is a powerful technique for image manipulation.

1-9 Creating a Mat from Submats
Problem

You would like to create a Mat manually from scratch, made of different submats.

Solution

setTo and **copyTo** are two important functions of OpenCV. setTo will set the color of all the pixels of a mat to the color specified, and copyTo will copy an existing Mat to another one. When using either setTo or copyTo you will probably work with submats, thus affecting only parts of the main mat.

To use setTo, we will use colors defined using OpenCV's Scalar object, which, for now, will be created with a set of values in the RGB color space. Let's see all this in action.

How it works

The first example will use setTo to create a mat made of submats, each of them of a different color.

Mat of Colored Submats

First, let's define the colors using RGB values. As mentioned, colors are created using a Scalar object, with three int values, where each value is between 0 and 255.

The first color is the blue intensity, the second is the green intensity, and the last one is the red intensity. Thus to create red, green, or blue, you put its main color value to its max intensity, so 255, and the others to 0.

See how it goes for red, green, and blue:

```
Scalar RED   = new Scalar(0, 0, 255); // Blue=0, Green=0, Red=255
Scalar GREEN = new Scalar(0, 255, 0); // Blue=0, Green=255, Red=0
Scalar BLUE  = new Scalar(255, 0, 0); // Blue=255, Green=0, Red=0
```

To define cyan, magenta, and yellow, let's think of those colors as the complementary colors of RGB, so we set the other channels to the max value of 255, and the main one to 0.

Cyan is complementary to red, so the red channel value is set to 0, and the other two channels are set to 255:

```
Scalar CYAN   = new Scalar(255, 255, 0);
```

Magenta is complementary to green, and yellow to blue. These are defined as follows:

```
Scalar MAGENTA = new Scalar(255, 0, 255);
Scalar YELLOW  = new Scalar(0, 255, 255);
```

Alright. We have the colors all set up; let's use them to create a mat of all the defined colors. The following setColors method takes the main mat object and fills a row with either the main RGB colors or the complementary colors CMY.

See how the submat content is filled using the setTo function on a submat with a scalar color.

```
static void setColors(Mat mat, boolean comp, int row) {
    for(int i = 0 ; i < 3 ; i ++) {
        Mat sub = mat.submat(row*100, row*100+100, i*100,
        i*100+100);
        if(comp) {   // RGB
          if(i==0) sub.setTo(RED);
          if(i==1) sub.setTo(GREEN);
```

```
      if(i==2) sub.setTo(BLUE);
    } else {     // CMY
      if(i==0) sub.setTo(CYAN);
      if(i==1) sub.setTo(MAGENTA);
      if(i==2) sub.setTo(YELLOW);
    }
  }
}
```

Then, the calling code creates the mat in three-channel RGB color mode and fills the first and second rows.

```
Mat mat = new Mat(200,300,CV_8UC3);
setColors(mat, false, 1);
setColors(mat, true, 0);
Imgcodecs.imwrite("output/rgbcmy.jpg", mat);
```

The result is a mat made of two rows, each of them filled with the created colored submats, as shown in Figure 1-18.

Figure 1-18. *Mat of colored submats*

Mat of Picture Submats

Colors are great, but you will probably be working with pictures. This second example is going to show you how to use submats filled with a picture content.

First start by creating a 200×200 mat and two submats: one for the top of the main mat, one for the bottom of the main mat.

```
int width = 200,height = 200;
Mat mat = new Mat(height,width,CV_8UC3);

Mat top = mat.submat(0,height/2,0,width);
Mat bottom = mat.submat(height/2,height,0,width);
```

Let's then create another small Mat by loading a picture into it and resizing it to the size of the top (or bottom) submat. Here you are introduced to the **resize** function of the **Imgproc** class.

```
Mat small = Imgcodecs.imread("images/kitten.jpg");
Imgproc.resize(small,small,top.size());
```

You are free to choose the picture, of course; for now, let's suppose the loaded small mat is like Figure 1-19:

Figure 1-19. *Kitten power*

The small cat mat is then copied to both the top and bottom submats.

Note that the preceding resize step is crucial; the copy succeeds because the small mat and the submat sizes are identical, and thus no problem occurs while copying.

```
small.copyTo(top);
small.copyTo(bottom);
Imgcodecs.imwrite("output/matofpictures.jpg", mat);
```

This gives a **matofpictures.jpg** file of two kittens as shown in Figure 1-20.

Figure 1-20. *Double kitten power*

If you forget to resize the small mat, the copy fails very badly, resulting in something like Figure 1-21.

Figure 1-21. *Kitten gone wrong*

1-10 Highlighting Objects in a Picture

Problem

You have a picture with a set of objects, animals, or shapes that you would like to highlight, maybe because you want to count them.

Solution

OpenCV offers a famous function named Canny, which can highlight lines in a picture. You will see how to use canny in more detail later in this chapter; for now, let's focus on the basic steps using Java.

OpenCV's canny works on gray mat for contour detection. While you can leave it to canny to do it for you, let's explicitly change the color space of the input mat to be in grayspace.

Changing color space is easily done with OpenCV using the **cvtColor** function found in the Core class.

How it works

Suppose you have a picture of tools as shown in Figure 1-22.

Figure 1-22. *Tools at work*

We start by loading the picture into a Mat as usual:

```
Mat tools = imread("images/tools.jpg");
```

We then convert the color of that tools mat using the **cvtColor** function, which takes a source mat, a target mat, and a target color space. Color space constants are found in the Imgproc class and have a prefix like **COLOR_**.

So to turn the mat to black and white, you can use the **COLOR_ RGB2GRAY** constant.

```
cvtColor(tools, tools, COLOR_RGB2GRAY);
```

The black-and-white picture is ready to be sent to **canny.** Parameters for the canny function are as follows:

- Source mat

- Target mat

- Low threshold: we will use 150.0

- High threshold: usually approximately low threshold*2 or low threshold*3

- Aperture: an odd value between 3 and 7; we will use 3. The higher the aperture, the more contours will be found.

- L2Gradient value, for now set to true

Canny computes a gradient value for each pixel, using a convolution matrix with the center pixels and neighboring pixels. If the gradient value is higher than the high threshold, then it is kept as an edge. If it's in between, it is kept if it has a high gradient connected to it.

Now, we can call the Canny function.

```
Canny(tools,tools,150.0,300.0,3,true);
imwrite("output/tools-01.png", target);
```

This outputs a picture as shown in Figure 1-23:

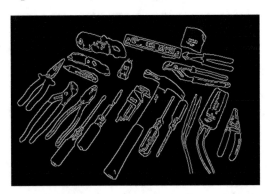

Figure 1-23. *Canny tools*

For the eyes, the printer, and the trees, it may be sometimes easier to draw the inverted Mat where white is turned to black, and black is turned to white. This is done using the **bitwise_not** function from the Core class.

```
Mat invertedTools = tools.clone();
bitwise_not(invertedTools, invertedTools);
imwrite("output/tools-02.png", invertedTools);
```

42

The result is shown in Figure 1-24.

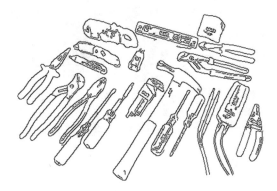

Figure 1-24. *Inverted canny tools*

You can of course apply the same **Canny** processing to ever more kitten pictures. Figures 1-25, 1-26, and 1-27 show the same code applied to a picture of kittens.

Figure 1-25. *Ready to be canny kittens*

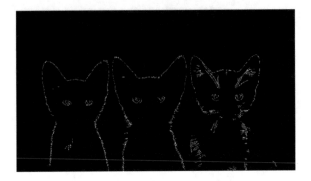

Figure 1-26. *Canny kittens*

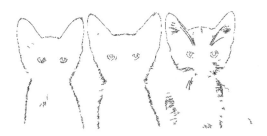

Figure 1-27. *Inverted canny kittens*

1-11 Using a Canny Result as a Mask

Problem

While canny is awesome at edge detection, another way of using its output is as a mask, which will give you a nice artistic image.

Let's experiment drawing the result of a canny operation on top of another picture.

Solutions

When performing a copy operation, you can use what is called a mask as a parameter. A mask is a regular one-channel Mat, thus with values of 0 and 1.

When performing a copy with a mask, if the mask value for that pixel is 0, the source mat pixel is not copied, and if the value is 1, the source pixel is copied to the target Mat.

How it works

In the previous recipe, from the result of the bitwise_not function we have obtained a new Mat object.

```
Mat kittens = imread("images/three_black_kittens.jpg");

cvtColor(kittens,kittens,COLOR_RGB2GRAY);
Canny(kittens,kittens,100.0,300.0,3, true);
bitwise_not(kittens,kittens);
```

If you decide to dump the kittens (probably not a good idea, because the file is pretty big...), you will see a bunch of zeros and ones; this is how the mask is created.

Now that we have the mask, let's create a white mat, named target, to be the target of the copy function.

```
Mat target = new Mat(kittens.height(), kittens.width(),
CV_8UC3, WHITE );
```

Then we load a source for the copy, and as you remember, we need to make sure it is of the same size as the other component of the copy operation, so target.

Let's perform a resize operation on the background object.

```
Mat bg = imread("images/light-blue-gradient.jpg");
Imgproc.resize(bg, bg, target.size());
```

There you go; you are ready for the copy.

```
bg.copyTo(target, kittens);
imwrite("output/kittens-03.png", target);
```

The resulting Mat is shown in Figure 1-28.

Figure 1-28. *Kittens on blue background*

Now can you answer the following question: Why are the cats drawn in white?

The correct answer is indeed that the underlying Mat was initialized to be all white; see the new Mat(…, WHITE) statement. When the mask prevents the copy of a pixel, that is, when its value for that pixel is zero, then the original color of the mat will show up, here WHITE, and this is how the kittens are shown in white in Figure 1-28. You could of course go ahead and try with a black underlying Mat, or a picture of your choice.

We will see some more of those examples in the coming chapters.

1-12 Detecting Edges with Contours

Problem

From the result of the canny operation, you would like to find a list of drawable contours, as well as drawing them on a Mat.

Solution

OpenCV has a set of two functions that often go hand in hand with the canny function: these functions are **findContours** and **drawContours**.

findContours takes a Mat and finds the edges, or the lines that define shapes, in that Mat. Since the original picture probably contains a lot of noise from colors and brightness, you usually use a preprocessed image, a black-and-white Mat where the canny function has been applied.

drawContours takes the results of **findContours**, a list of contour objects, and allows you to draw them with specific features, like the thickness of the line used to draw and the color.

How it works

As presented in the solution, OpenCV's findContours method takes a preprocessed picture along with other parameters:

1. The preprocessed Mat

2. An empty List that will receive the contour object (MatOfPoint)

3. A hierarchy Mat; you can ignore this for now and leave it as an empty Mat

4. The contour retrieval mode, for example whether to create relationship between contours or return all of them

5. The type of approximation used to store the contours; for example, draw all the points or only key defining points

First, let's wrap the preprocessing of the original picture, and the finding contours, in our own custom method, **find_contours**.

```
static List find_contours(Mat image, boolean onBlank) {
    Mat imageBW = new Mat();

    Imgproc.cvtColor(image, imageBW, Imgproc.COLOR_BGR2GRAY);
    Canny(imageBW,imageBW,100.0,300.0,3, true);

    List contours = new ArrayList<MatOfPoint>();
    Imgproc.findContours(imageBW, contours, new Mat(),
            Imgproc.RETR_LIST,
            Imgproc.CHAIN_APPROX_SIMPLE);

    return contours;
}
```

This method returns the list of found contours, where each contour is itself a list of points, or in OpenCV terms, a MatOfPoint object.

Next, we write a **draw_contours** method that will take the original Mat to find out the size of each contours found in the previous step, and the thickness we want each contour to be drawn with.

To draw the contours à la opencv, you usually use a for loop and give the index of the contour to draw to the drawContours method.

```
static Mat draw_contours(Mat originalMat, List contours,
int thickness) {
    Mat target =
```

```
    new Mat(originalMat.height(), originalMat.width(),
    CV_8UC3, WHITE);

  for (int i = 0; i < contours.size(); i++)
    Imgproc.drawContours(target, contours, i, BLACK, thickness);

  return target;
}
```

Great; the building blocks of this recipe have been written so you can put them in action. You can use the same picture of kittens as before as the base picture.

```
Mat kittens = imread("images/three_black_kittens.jpg");
List contours = find_contours(kittens, true);

Mat target = draw_contours(kittens, contours, 7);
imwrite("output/kittens-contours-7.png", target);
```

The draw_contours result is shown in Figure 1-29.

Figure 1-29. *Kitten contours, thickness=7*

Go ahead and change the thickness used when drawing contours. For example, with the thickness set to 3, the slightly different result, with thinner lines, is shown in Figure 1-30.

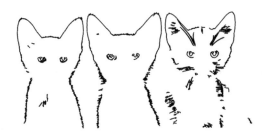

Figure 1-30. *Kitten contours, thickness=3*

From there, we can again use the resulting Mat as a mask when doing a background copy.

The following snippet is code taken from the previous recipe; the function takes a mask and does a copy using that mask.

```
static Mat mask_on_bg(Mat mask, String backgroundFilePath) {
    Mat target = new Mat(mask.height(),mask.
    width(),CV_8UC3,WHITE);
    Mat bg = imread(backgroundFilePath);
    Imgproc.resize(bg, bg, target.size());
    bg.copyTo(target, mask);
    return target;
}
```

Figure 1-31 shows the result of a copy with the mask created while drawing contours on thickness set to 3.

Figure 1-31. *White kittens on blue background*

Notably in Chapter 3, you will be introduced to cooler ways of using masks and backgrounds for some artsy results, but for now, let's wrap this recipe up.

1-13 Working with Video Streams

Problem

You would like to use OpenCV on a video stream and do image processing in real time.

Solution

The Java version of OpenCV presents a videoio package, and in particular a **VideoCapture** object, that provides ways to read a Mat object directly from a connected video device.

You will see first how to retrieve a Mat object from the video device, with a given size, and then save the Mat to a file.

Using a Frame, you will also see how to plug previous processing code in the real-time image acquisition.

How it works

Taking Still Pictures

Let's introduce the do_still_captures function. It will take a number of frames to grab, how much time to wait between each frame, and which camera_id to take pictures from.

A camera_id is the index of the capture device connected to your machine. You would usually use 0, but you may come to plug in and use other external devices, and in that case, use the corresponding camera_id.

First a VideoCapture object is created, with the camera_id in parameter.

Then you create a blank Mat object and pass it to receive data from the **camera.read()** function.

The Mat object is the standard OpenCV Mat object you have worked with up to now, and so you can easily apply the same transformations you have learned.

For now, let's simply save the frames one by one, with timestamped file names.

Once finished, you can put the camera back to standby mode with the **release** method on the VideoCapture object.

See how it goes in the following listing.

```
static void do_still_captures(int frames, int lapse, int
camera_id) {

        VideoCapture camera = new VideoCapture(camera_id);
        camera.set(Videoio.CV_CAP_PROP_FRAME_WIDTH, 320);
        camera.set(Videoio.CV_CAP_PROP_FRAME_HEIGHT, 240);

        Mat frame = new Mat();
        for(int i = 0 ; i <frames;i++) {
```

```
    if (camera.read(frame)){
        String filename = "video/"+new Date()+".jpg";
        Imgcodecs.imwrite(filename, frame);
        try {Thread.sleep(lapse*1000);}
        catch (Exception e) {e.printStackTrace();}
    }
}

    camera.release();
}
```

Calling the newly created function is simply a matter of filling the parameters, and so the following will take ten pictures from device with ID 0, and will wait 1 second between each shot.

```
do_still_captures(10,1,0);
```

As is shown in Figure 1-32, ten pictures should be created in the video folder of the project. And, indeed, time flies; it is already past midnight.

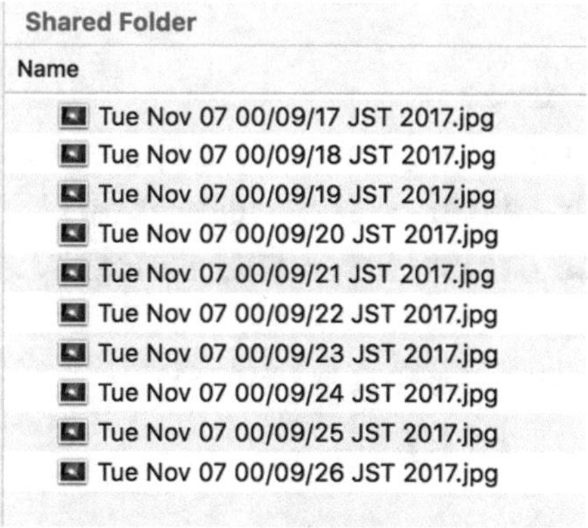

Shared Folder
Name
🔳 Tue Nov 07 00/09/17 JST 2017.jpg
🔳 Tue Nov 07 00/09/18 JST 2017.jpg
🔳 Tue Nov 07 00/09/19 JST 2017.jpg
🔳 Tue Nov 07 00/09/20 JST 2017.jpg
🔳 Tue Nov 07 00/09/21 JST 2017.jpg
🔳 Tue Nov 07 00/09/22 JST 2017.jpg
🔳 Tue Nov 07 00/09/23 JST 2017.jpg
🔳 Tue Nov 07 00/09/24 JST 2017.jpg
🔳 Tue Nov 07 00/09/25 JST 2017.jpg
🔳 Tue Nov 07 00/09/26 JST 2017.jpg

Figure 1-32. *Mini–time lapse of still bedroom*

Working in Real Time

Alright; so the bad news here is that the OpenCV Java wrapper does not include obvious ways to convert a Mat to a BufferedImage, which is the de facto object to work with images in the Java graphic packages.

Without going into much detail here, let's say you actually need this **MatToBufferedImage** to work in real time in a Java frame, by converting a Mat object to a BufferedImage and thus being able to render it into standard Java GUI objects.

Let's quickly write a method that converts an OpenCV Mat object to a standard Java BufferedImage.

```
public static BufferedImage MatToBufferedImage(Mat frame) {
    int type = 0;
    if(frame==null) return null;
    if (frame.channels() == 1) {
        type = BufferedImage.TYPE_BYTE_GRAY;
    } else if (frame.channels() == 3) {
        type = BufferedImage.TYPE_3BYTE_BGR;
    }
    BufferedImage image =
        new BufferedImage(frame.width(), frame.height(), type);
    WritableRaster raster = image.getRaster();
    DataBufferByte dataBuffer = (DataBufferByte) raster.
    getDataBuffer();
    byte[] data = dataBuffer.getData();
    frame.get(0, 0, data);
    return image;
}
```

Once you have this building block of code, it actually gets easier, but you will still need one more glue piece of code; a custom panel that extends the Java Panel class JPanel.

What this custom panel, which we will call **MatPanel**, is made of is a field which is the Mat object to draw. Then MatPanel extends the Java JPanel class in a way that the **paint()** method now converts the Mat directly using the method you have just seen before: **MatToBufferedImage**.

```
class MatPanel extends JPanel {
    public Mat mat;

    public void paint(Graphics g) {
        g.drawImage(WebcamExample.MatToBufferedImage(mat), 0,
        0, this);
    }
}
```

Alright; the somehow missing code in the default OpenCV packages has now been reimplemented and you can create a Java frame ready to receive Mat objects.

```
MatPanel t = new MatPanel();
JFrame frame0 = new JFrame();
frame0.getContentPane().add(t);
frame0.setDefaultCloseOperation(JFrame.DISPOSE_ON_CLOSE);
frame0.setSize(320, 240);
frame0.setVisible(true);
frame0.setDefaultCloseOperation(JFrame.EXIT_ON_CLOSE);
```

The final step of this exercise is to simply use code similar to the **do_ still_captures** method, but instead of stopping after a number of frames, you will write a forever loop to give the video streaming impression.

```
VideoCapture camera = new VideoCapture(0);
camera.set(Videoio.CV_CAP_PROP_FRAME_WIDTH, 320);
camera.set(Videoio.CV_CAP_PROP_FRAME_HEIGHT, 240);
Mat frame = new Mat();
```

```
while(true){
  if (camera.read(frame)){
    t.mat=frame;
    t.repaint();
  }
}
```

Figure 1-33 gives a real-time view of a Japanese room at 1 am, painted in real time in a Java frame.

Figure 1-33. *Real-time stream in Java frame*

Obviously, the goal of this is to be able to work with the Mat object in real time, so now a good exercise for you is to write the necessary code that leads to the screenshot seen in Figure 1-34.

Figure 1-34. *Canny picture in real time*

The answer is shown in the following code snippet, and as you would have guessed, this is a simple matter of applying the already seen **canny** transformation to the Mat object read from the camera.

```
if (camera.read(frame)){
    Imgproc.cvtColor(frame,frame, Imgproc.COLOR_RGB2GRAY);
    Mat target = new Mat();
    Imgproc.Canny(frame,target,100.0,150.0,3,true);
    t.mat=target;
t.repaint();
}
```

1-14 Writing OpenCV Code in Scala

Problem

Now that you can write a bit of OpenCV code in Java, you are starting to enjoy it, but would like to use Scala instead to reduce boilerplate code.

Solution

The current OpenCV setup you have done so far makes it easy to run any class compiled for the JavaVM. So if you manage to compile Scala classes, and there is a Leiningen plug-in just for that, then the rest is pretty much identical.

What that means is that with the current Leiningen setup you have used so far, you will just need to update the project metadata, in **project.clj**, in a few places to get things going.

This works in two steps. First, add the scala compiler and libraries, and then update the directory where the files with scala code are found.

How it works

Basic Setup

The **project.clj** needs be updated in a few places as highlighted in the following.

- The project name; that is optional, of course.

- The main class; you may keep the same name, but if you do, make sure to delete the old Java code with **lein clean**.

- Next, the lein-zinc plug-in is the all-in-one scala plug-in for Leiningen and needs to be added.

- The lein-zinc plug-in needs to be triggered before lein performs compilation, so we will add a step to the **prep-tasks** key of the project metadata. The prep-tasks key is responsible for defining tasks that need to be executed before similar commands run.

- Finally, the scala library dependency is added to the dependencies key.

The resulting project.clj file can be found in the following.

```
(defproject opencv-scala-fun "0.1.0-SNAPSHOT"
  :java-source-paths ["scala"]
  :repositories [["vendredi"
    "http://hellonico.info:8081/repository/hellonico/"]]
  :main SimpleOpenCV
  :plugins [
  [lein-zinc "1.2.0"]
  [lein-auto "0.1.3"]]
  :prep-tasks ["zinc" "compile"]
  :auto {:default {:file-pattern #"\.(scala)$"}}
  :dependencies [
   [org.clojure/clojure "1.8.0"]
   [org.scala-lang/scala-library "2.12.4"]
   [opencv/opencv "3.3.1"]
   [opencv/opencv-native "3.3.1"]
])
```

Your new project file setup for scala should look something like the structure shown in Figure 1-35.

Figure 1-35. *Scala project directory structure*

As you can see, not so much is changed from the Java setup, but make sure your source files are in the scala folder now.

To confirm that the whole thing is in place and set up properly, let's try a simplistic OpenCV example again, but this time in Scala.

You will need to load the OpenCV native library as was done before in the Java examples. If you put the loadLibrary call anywhere in the scala object definition, it will be treated as a static call for the JVM and will load the library when loading the newly Scala written SimpleOpenCV class.

The rest of the code is a rather direct translation of the Java code.

```
import org.opencv.core._
import org.opencv.core.CvType._
import clojure.lang.RT.loadLibrary

object SimpleOpenCV {
    loadLibrary(Core.NATIVE_LIBRARY_NAME)
    def main(args: Array[String]) {
      val mat = Mat.eye(3, 3, CV_8UC1)
      println("mat = \n" + mat.dump())
    }
}
```

When compiling the preceding code, some Java bytecode is generated from the scala sources, in the target folder, in the same way it was done with the Java code.

Thus, you can run the scala code in the exact same way as you were doing with Java, or in command terms:

```
lein auto run
```

The output in the console shows the expected OpenCV 3x3 eye mat dumped onscreen.

```
NikoMacBook% lein auto run

auto> Files changed: scala/DrawingContours.scala, scala/
SimpleOpenCV.scala, scala/SimpleOpenCV1.scala, scala/
SimpleOpenCV2.scala, scala/SimpleOpenCV3.scala
auto> Running: lein run
scala version:  2.12.4
sbt    version:  0.13.9
fork java?       false
[warn] Pruning sources from previous analysis, due to
incompatible CompileSetup.
mat =
[  1,   0,   0;
   0,   1,   0;
   0,   0,   1]

auto> Completed.
```

An overview of the updated setup in Atom for scala can be found in Figure 1-36.

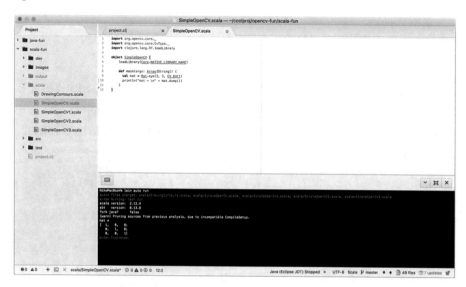

Figure 1-36. *Scala setup*

Blurred

Agreed, the first Scala example was a little bit too simple, so let's use some of the power of the OpenCV blurring effect in Scala now.

```scala
import clojure.lang.RT.loadLibrary
import org.opencv.core._
import org.opencv.imgcodecs.Imgcodecs._
import org.opencv.imgproc.Imgproc._

object SimpleOpenCV2 {
  loadLibrary(Core.NATIVE_LIBRARY_NAME)

  def main(args: Array[String]) {
    val neko = imread("images/bored-cat.jpg")
    imwrite("output/blurred_cat.png", blur_(neko, 20))
  }
  def blur_(input: Mat, numberOfTimes:Integer) : Mat = {
    for(_ <- 1 to numberOfTimes )
      blur(input, input, new Size(11.0, 11.0))
    input
  }
}
```

As you can see, the blur effect is called successively many times in a row to incrementally apply the blur effect on the same Mat object.

And the bored cat from Figure 1-37 can be blurred to a blurred bored cat in Figure 1-38.

Figure 1-37. *Bored cat*

Figure 1-38. *Blurred and bored*

Surely you have tried this on your local machine and found two things that are quite nice with the scala setup.

Compilation times are reduced a bit, and it is actually quicker to see your OpenCV code in action. The scala compiler seems to determine the required compilation steps from incremental code changes.

Also, static imports, even though they exist already in Java, seem to be more naturally integrated with the scala setup.

Canny Effect

In an effort to reduce boilerplate code a little bit more, Scala makes it easy to import not only classes but also methods.

This third example in the scala recipe will show how to apply the canny transformation after changing the color space of a loaded OpenCV Mat.

The code is quite clean; the only sad part is that the OpenCV function **vconcat** is expecting a java.util.Array and cannot take native scala objects as parameters, and so you'll need to use the **Arrays.asList** Java function instead.

```
import java.util.Arrays
import org.opencv.core._
import org.opencv.core.CvType._
import org.opencv.core.Core._
import org.opencv.imgproc.Imgproc._
import org.opencv.imgcodecs.Imgcodecs._
import clojure.lang.RT.loadLibrary

object SimpleOpenCV3 {
    loadLibrary(Core.NATIVE_LIBRARY_NAME)

    def main(args: Array[String]) {
      val cat = imread("images/cat3.jpg")

      cvtColor(cat,cat,COLOR_RGB2GRAY)
      Canny(cat,cat, 220.0,230.0,5,true)

      val cat2 = cat.clone()
      bitwise_not(cat2,cat2)
      val target = new Mat
      vconcat(Arrays.asList(cat,cat2), target)

      imwrite("output/canny-cat.png", target)
    }
}
```

The canny parameters have been taken to output something in the simple art space, and this time it's not really effective to find out edges at all. Figures 1-39 and 1-40 show the before/after of the canny effect on a loaded cat image.

Figure 1-39. *Not afraid of Scala*

Figure 1-40. *I has been warned*

The Drawing contours example written for Java has also been ported to Scala and is available in the source code of the samples available with this book; for now, this is left as a simple exercise to the reader.

1-15 Writing OpenCV Code in Kotlin
Problems

Writing OpenCV transformations in Scala was quite exciting, but now that Google is pushing for Kotlin you would like to be like the new kids on the block and write OpenCV code in Kotlin.

Solutions

Of course, there is also a Kotlin plug-in for Leiningen. As for the scala setup, you will need to update the project metadata, again the file **project.clj**.

You will mostly need to add the Kotlin plug-in, as well as the path to the Kotlin source files.

How it works
Basic Setup

The places to update in the project.clj file are very similar to those for the updates required for the scala setup and have been highlighted in the following snippet.

```
(defproject opencv-kotlin-fun "0.1.0-SNAPSHOT"
  :repositories [
  ["vendredi" "http://hellonico.info:8081/repository/
  hellonico/"]]
  :main First
  :plugins [
  [hellonico/lein-kotlin "0.0.2.1"]
  [lein-auto "0.1.3"]]
```

```
:prep-tasks ["javac" "compile" "kotlin" ]
:kotlin-source-path "kotlin"
:java-source-paths ["kotlin"]
:auto {:default {:file-pattern #"\.(kt)$"}}
:dependencies [
 [org.clojure/clojure "1.8.0"]
 [opencv/opencv "3.3.1"]
 [opencv/opencv-native "3.3.1"]])
```

Since the Kotlin classes are compiled to JavaVM bytecode transparently by the plug-in, you can refer to the compiled classes as you have done up to now.

Obviously, the first test is to find out whether you can load a Mat object and dump its nice zero and one values.

The following ultrashort Kotlin snippet does just that.

```
import org.opencv.core.*
import org.opencv.core.CvType.*
import clojure.lang.RT

object First {
    @JvmStatic fun main(args: Array<String>) {
        RT.loadLibrary(Core.NATIVE_LIBRARY_NAME)
        val mat = Mat.eye(3, 3, CV_8UC1)
        println(mat.dump())
    }
}
```

The First.kt file should be in the Kotlin folder before you run the usual Leiningen run command.

```
lein auto run -m First
```

And the command output, showing the OpenCV object properly created and printed on the console, is also necessary.

```
auto> Files changed: kotlin/Blurring.kt, kotlin/ColorMapping.
kt, kotlin/First.kt, kotlin/ui/World0.kt, kotlin/ui/World1.kt,
kotlin/ui/World2.kt, kotlin/ui/World3.kt, kotl
in/ui/World4.kt
auto> Running: lein run -m First
[  1,    0,    0;
   0,    1,    0;
   0,    0,    1]
auto> Completed.
```

That was an easy one. Let's see how to do something slightly more complex with Kotlin and OpenCV.

Color Mapping

The following new example shows how to switch between different color maps using the **applyColorMap** function of **Imgproc**, everything now coded in Kotlin.

```kotlin
import org.opencv.core.*
import org.opencv.imgproc.Imgproc.*
import org.opencv.imgcodecs.Imgcodecs.*

object ColorMapping {
    @JvmStatic fun main(args: Array<String>) {
        System.loadLibrary(Core.NATIVE_LIBRARY_NAME)

        val mat = imread("resources/kitten.jpg")

        applyColorMap(mat,mat,COLORMAP_WINTER)
        imwrite("output/winter.png", mat)
```

```
applyColorMap(mat,mat,COLORMAP_BONE)
imwrite("output/bone.png", mat)

applyColorMap(mat,mat,COLORMAP_HOT)
val mat2 = mat.clone()
val newSize =
    Size((mat.width()/2).toDouble(),(mat.height()/2).
    toDouble())
resize(mat2,mat2,newSize)

imwrite("output/hot.png", mat2)
    }
}
```

As you may know, constructor calls in Kotlin do not need the verbose **new** keyword, and just like in Scala, methods can be statically imported.

You can see this in action and with the original input image in Figure 1-41.

Figure 1-41. *Cat ready for anything*

You can see three files being created; those three output files are shown in Figures 1-42, 1-43, and 1-44.

Figure 1-42. Bone cat

Figure 1-43. Winter cat

Figure 1-44. Hot cat, changed its size

Proper type conversion seems to be a bit challenging in Kotlin, but the code is again very compact and just like in Scala removes quite a bit of boilerplate code.

User Interface

One main reason you may want to use Kotlin is for its quite incredible tornadofx library, which make it easier to write simple user interface in the JVM underlying GUI framework JavaFX.

Small applications like this are quite useful to give the user the chance to change OpenCV parameters and see the results in pseudo–real time.

Kotlin Setup

The tornadofx library can be added to the **project.clj** file in the dependencies section, like the extracted snippet in the following:

```
(defproject opencv-kotlin-fun "0.1.0-SNAPSHOT"
  ...
  :dependencies [
  [org.clojure/clojure "1.8.0"]
  [opencv/opencv "3.3.1"]
  [no.tornado/tornadofx "1.7.11"]
  [opencv/opencv-native "3.3.1"]])
```

Since the goal of this recipe is to give you ideas of creativity, we are not going to get deep into learning how to write Kotlin code and write Kotlin code with tornadofx. But you will quickly enjoy a few Kotlin examples on how to integrate those with OpenCV.

The coming first example shows you how to bootstrap your Kotlin code to show an image within a frame.

UI for Dummies

A simple tornadofx application basically follows a given Launcher ➤ App ➤ View structure, as shown in the graph of Figure 1-45.

71

```
                                                    MyView(Class)
  FX Launcher   ---►  MyApp(Class)   ---►             extends
                                                        View
```

Figure 1-45. *Tornadofx application graph*

With this diagram in mind, we need to create three classes.

- HelloWorld0: the main view of the User Interface application

- MyApp0: the JavaFX application object to send to the JavaFX launcher

- World0: the main class, created only once, thus using object instead of class to define it, to start the JVM-based application

A view in tornadofx is made of a root panel, which can be customized with the javafx widgets as you want.

- The following code creates a single view, where the view is composed of an image embedded with the imageview widget.

- The size of the image of the imageview is set within the block defining the widget.

- The view initialization is done in the **init {..}** block, and the root object, since it cannot be instantiated again, is using the magical function **with**.

```
package ui;

import tornadofx.*
import javafx.application.Application
import javafx.scene.layout.*

class HelloWorld0 : View() {
    override val root = VBox()
```

```
init {
    with(root) {
        imageview("cat.jpg") {
            fitHeight = 160.0
            fitWidth = 200.0
        }
    }
}
}
```

The rest of the code is standard tornadofx/javafx boilerplate to start the JavaFX-based application properly.

```
class MyApp0: App(HelloWorld0::class)
```

```
object World0 {
    @JvmStatic fun main(args: Array<String>) {
        Application.launch(MyApp0::class.java, *args)
    }
}
```

Running the preceding code with leiningen in auto mode is done as you have done up to now with

```
lein auto run -m ui.World0
```

And a graphical frame should show up on your screen (Figure 1-46).

Figure 1-46. *Image in frame*

Actually, the code and the frame are slightly different. A title was set in the root block with the following snippet added at the proper location. You should find out where!

```
title = "Image in Frame"
```

UI with Reactive Buttons

The next example builds on the previous one and adds a button that when clicked increments an internal counter, and the value of that counter is then displayed onscreen in real time.

A reactive value can be created with a **SimpleIntegerProperty**, or SimpleXXXProperty from the **javafx.beans** package.

That reactive value can then bound to a widget, and in the coming example it will be bound to a label, so that the value of the label is equal to the value of the property.

A button is a simple UI widget on which you can define an action handler. The handler code can be either inside the block or in a different Kotlin function.

With the goal and explanation in place, let's go to the following code snippet.

```
package ui;

import tornadofx.*
import javafx.application.Application
import javafx.scene.layout.*
import javafx.beans.property.SimpleIntegerProperty
import javafx.geometry.Pos

class CounterView : View() {
  override val root = BorderPane()
  val counter = SimpleIntegerProperty()
```

```
init {
  title = "Counter"

  with (root) {
    style {
      padding = box(20.px)
    }

    center {
      vbox(10.0) {
        alignment = Pos.CENTER

        label() {
          bind(counter)
          style { fontSize = 25.px }
        }

        button("Click to increment") {
          action {increment()} }}}}}
  fun increment() {counter.value += 1}
}

class CounterApp : App(CounterView::class)

object Counter {
  @JvmStatic fun main(args: Array<String>) {
    Application.launch(CounterApp::class.java, *args)
  }
}
```

The result of running the counter application is shown in Figure 1-47.

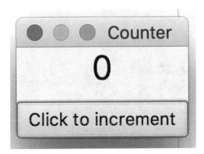

Figure 1-47. *Simple counter app*

And after a few clicks on the beautiful button, you will get something as in Figure 1-48.

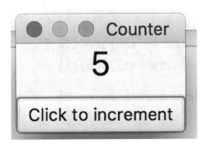

Figure 1-48. *A few button clicks to increase the counter*

Blurring Application

Well, that was cool, but it looked like a course on creating GUI, and had not much to do with OpenCV.

Right.

So, this last Kotlin application builds on the two previous examples and shows how to build a blurring application, where the amount of blur is set by a reactive property.

You have to go back and forth between the Image object of the Java land and the Mat object of the OpenCV land. The following example shows a quick way of doing this by using the **imencode** function from OpenCV, which encodes a Mat object to bytes without turning all this to a file.

The blurring application has a val of type SimpleObjectProperty, which when changes as its graphical view is being updated.

The longer list of imports is a bit annoying, but you would probably not need much more of those for your own custom application.

```
package ui.cv;

import org.opencv.core.*
import org.opencv.imgproc.Imgproc.*
import org.opencv.imgcodecs.Imgcodecs.*
import clojure.lang.RT
import tornadofx.*
import javafx.application.Application
import javafx.scene.layout.*
import javafx.scene.paint.Color
import javafx.application.Platform
import javafx.beans.property.SimpleIntegerProperty
import javafx.beans.property.SimpleObjectProperty
import javafx.geometry.Pos
import javafx.scene.image.Image

class CounterView : View() {
    override val root = BorderPane()
    val counter = SimpleIntegerProperty(1)
    val imageObj = SimpleObjectProperty(Image("/cat.jpg"))
    val source = imread("images/cat.jpg")

    init {
        title = "Blur"
        with (root) {
```

```
style {
    padding = box(20.px)
}
center {
    vbox(10.0) {
        alignment = Pos.CENTER
        label() {
            bind(counter)
            style { fontSize = 25.px }
        }
        imageview(imageObj) {
            fitWidth = 150.0
            fitHeight = 100.0
        }
        button("Click to increment") {
                action {
              increment()
                randomImage()
                }
        }
        button("Click to decrement {
                action {
              decrement()
              randomImage()
                }
        }
    }
}
}
}
```

```
fun blurImage() {
    val result_mat = Mat()
    blur(source, result_mat,
        Size(counter.value.toDouble(),counter.value.
        toDouble()))
    val mat_of_bytes = MatOfByte()
    imencode(".jpg", result_mat, mat_of_bytes)
    imageObj.value =
        Image(java.io.ByteArrayInputStream(mat_of_bytes.
        toArray()))
}

fun increment() {
    counter.value += 6
}

fun decrement() {
    if(counter.value>6)
        counter.value -= 6
}
}

class MyBlurApp : App(CounterView::class)
object Blur {
    @JvmStatic fun main(args: Array<String>) {
        RT.loadLibrary(Core.NATIVE_LIBRARY_NAME)
        Application.launch(MyBlurApp::class.java, *args)
    }
}
```

As usual, Leiningen takes care of doing all the Kotlin compilation automatically for you on file change, and the blurring application appears as in Figure 1-49.

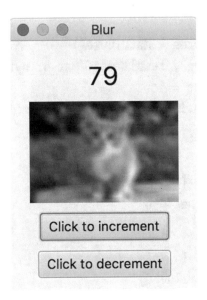

Figure 1-49. *Blurring application*

When you click the increment button, the cat image becomes more blurred, and when you click decrement, it becomes smoother again.

There are a few more tornadofx examples in the code samples along with this book, so do not hesitate to check them out. You will probably get more UI with OpenCV ideas; for example a drag-and-drop panel of images, when images can be blurred at will. Doesn't sound that out of reach anymore, does it?

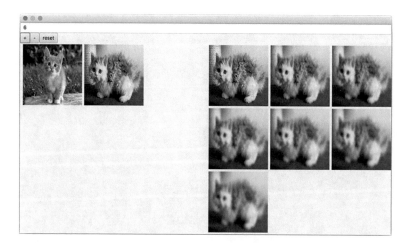

The first chapter has been filled with recipes, starting from creating a small project in OpenCV on the JavaVM, working through gradually more complicated image manipulation examples, first in Java, and then finally enjoying the JavaVM runtime environment and thus working with Scala and then Kotlin code with the expressive tornadofx library.

The door is now wide open to introduce the origami library, which is a Clojure wrapper for OpenCV. The environment will bring you even more concise code and more interactiveness to try new things and be creative. Time to get excited.

> *I have a general sense of excitement about the future, and I don't know what that looks like yet. But it will be whatever I make it.*
>
> Amanda Lindhout

CHAPTER 2

OpenCV with Origami

After staring at origami directions long enough, you sort of become one with them and start understanding them from the inside.

Zooey Deschanel

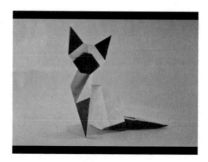

The Origami library was born out of the motivation that computer vision-related programming should be simple to set up, simple to keep running, and easy to experiment with.

These days, when artificial intelligence and neural networks are all the rage, I was on a mission to prepare and generate data for various neural networks. It quickly became clear that you cannot just dump any kind of image or video data to a network and expect it to behave efficiently. You need to organize all those images or videos by size, maybe colors or content, and automate the processing of images as much as possible,

N. Modrzyk, *Java Image Processing Recipes*, https://doi.org/10.1007/978-1-4842-3465-5_2

because sorting those one billion images by hand may prove time consuming indeed.

So, in this chapter we present Origami, a Clojure wrapper, a project template, and samples to work with for the OpenCV library on the JavaVM, all of this working with a concise language.

The examples will be done in such a way that you will be introduced to the OpenCV code via Clojure.

The setup you have seen in the previous chapter can be almost entirely reused as is, so no time will be wasted learning what was already learned. Mainly, you will just need to add the library as a dependency to a newly created project.

Once this simple additional setup is done, we will review OpenCV concepts through the eyes of the Origami library.

2-1 Starting to Code with Origami

Life itself is simple…it's just not easy.

Steve Maraboli

Problem

You have heard about this library wrapping OpenCV in a lightweight DSL named Origami and you would like to install it and give it a try on your machine.

Solution

If you have read or flipped through the first chapter of this book, you will remember that Leiningen was used to create a project template and lay out files in a simple project layout.

Here, you will use a different project template named clj-opencv, which will download the dependencies and copy the required files for you.

You will then be presented with the different coding styles that can be used with this new setup.

How it works

With Leiningen still installed on your machine, you can create a new project based on a template in the same way used for creating a Java opencv-based project.

Project Setup with a Leiningen Template

The project template this time is named clj-opencv and is called with Leiningen using the following one-liner on the terminal or console:

```
lein new clj-opencv myfirstcljcv
```

This will download the new template and create a myfirstcljcv folder with approximately the following content:

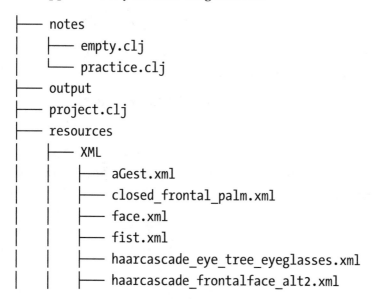

```
├── notes
│   ├── empty.clj
│   └── practice.clj
├── output
├── project.clj
├── resources
│   ├── XML
│   │   ├── aGest.xml
│   │   ├── closed_frontal_palm.xml
│   │   ├── face.xml
│   │   ├── fist.xml
│   │   ├── haarcascade_eye_tree_eyeglasses.xml
│   │   ├── haarcascade_frontalface_alt2.xml
```

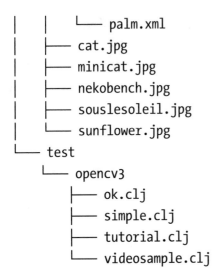

```
|    |      └── palm.xml
|    ├── cat.jpg
|    ├── minicat.jpg
|    ├── nekobench.jpg
|    ├── souslesoleil.jpg
|    └── sunflower.jpg
└── test
    └── opencv3
        ├── ok.clj
        ├── simple.clj
        ├── tutorial.clj
        └── videosample.clj
```

6 directories, 19 files

In the preceding file structure

- notes is a folder containing code in the form of notes, for gorilla and lein-gorilla. We will review how to use those two beasts right after.

- project.clj is the already seen leiningen project file.

- resources contains sample images and XML files for exercising and opencv recognition feature.

- test contains sample Clojure code showing how to get started with opencv and origami.

The project.clj file, as you remember, holds almost all of the project metadata. This time we will use a version that is slightly updated from what you have seen in Chapter 1.

The main differences from the previous chapter are highlighted in the following, so let's review it quickly.

```
(defproject sample5 "0.1-SNAPSHOT"
:injections [
 (clojure.lang.RT/loadLibrary org.opencv.core.Core/NATIVE_
LIBRARY_NAME)]
:plugins [[lein-gorilla "0.4.0"]]
:test-paths ["test"]
:resource-paths ["rsc"]
:main opencv3.ok
:repositories [
  ["vendredi" "https://repository.hellonico.info/repository/
hellonico/"]]
:aliases {"notebook" ["gorilla" ":ip" "0.0.0.0" ":port" "10000"]}
:profiles {:dev {
  :resource-paths ["resources"]
  :dependencies [
  ; used for proto repl
  [org.clojure/tools.nrepl "0.2.11"]
  ; proto repl
  [proto-repl "0.3.1"]
  ; use to start a gorilla repl
  [gorilla-repl "0.4.0"]
  [seesaw "1.4.5"]]}}
:dependencies [
 [org.clojure/clojure "1.8.0"]
 [org.clojure/tools.cli "0.3.5"]
 [origami "0.1.2"]])
```

As expected, the origami library has been added as a dependency in the dependencies section.

A plug-in named gorilla has also been added. This will help you run python's notebook style code; we will cover that later on in this recipe.

The injections segment may be a bit obscure at first, but it mostly says that the loading of the native OpenCV library will be done on starting the environment, so you do not have to repeat it in all the examples, as was the problem in the first chapter.

Everything Is OK

The main namespace to run is **opencv3.ok**; let's run it right now to make sure the setup is ready. This has not changed from the first chapter, and you still use the same command on the terminal or console to load code with:

```
lein run
```

After a short bit of output, you should be able to see something like

```
Using OpenCV Version:  3.3.1-dev ..
#object[org.opencv.core.Mat 0x69ce2f62 Mat [ 1200*1600*CV_8UC1,
isCont=true, isSubmat=false, nativeObj=0x7fcb16cefa70,
dataAddr=0x10f203000 ]]
A new gray neko has arisen!
```

The file grey-neko.jpg would have been created in the project folder and be like the picture in Figure 2-1.

Figure 2-1. *Grey Neko*

The code of the **opencv3.ok** namespace is written in full as follows:

```
(ns opencv3.ok
    (:require [opencv3.core :refer :all]))

(defn -main [& args]
  (println "Using OpenCV Version: " VERSION "..")
  (->
  (imread "resources/cat.jpg")
  (cvt-color! COLOR_RGB2GRAY)
  (imwrite "grey-neko.jpg")
  (println "A new gray neko has arisen!")))
```

You would recognize the **imread**, **cvtColor**, **imwrite** opencv functions used in the previous chapter, and indeed the java opencv functions are simply wrapped in Clojure.

This first code sequence flow written in the origami DSL is shown in Figure 2-2.

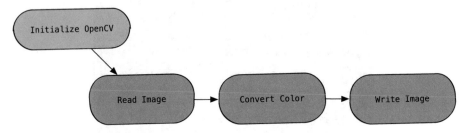

Figure 2-2. *Code flow from the first Origami example*

Webcam Check

If you have a webcam plugged in, there is another sample that starts the camera and stream in a video. The file to run this is in **samplevideo.clj**.

As before, you can start the sample by specifying the namespace to the lein run command.

```
lein run -m opencv3.videosample
```

When the command starts, you will be presented with a moving view of the coffee shop you are typing those few lines of code in, just as in Figure 2-3.

Figure 2-3. *Tokyo coffee shop*

While this was just to run the examples included with the project template, you can already start writing your own experimental code in your own files and run them using the lein run command.

The Auto Plug-in Strikes Back

You will see soon why this is usually not the best way to work with origami, because this recompiles all your source files each time. This is however a technique that can be used to check that all your code compiles and runs without errors.

So here is a quick reminder on how to set up the auto plug-in solution presented in Chapter 1 for Java, Scala, and Kotlin, this time for Clojure/ Origami code.

Modify the **project.clj** file to add the lein-auto plug-in so it matches the following code:

```
:plugins [[lein-gorilla "0.4.0"][lein-auto "0.1.3"]]
:auto {:default {:file-pattern #"\.(clj)$"}}
```

This is not in the project template by default because it's probably not needed most of the time.

Once you have added this, you can run the usual auto command by prefixing the command you want to execute with auto. Here:

```
lein auto run
```

This will execute the main namespace and wait for the file change to compile and execute again.

And so, after modifying the main method of the **ok.clj** file like in the following:

```
(defn -main [& args]
    (->
     (imread "resources/cat.jpg")
     (cvt-color! COLORMAP_JET)
     (imwrite "jet-neko.jpg")
     (println "A new jet neko has arisen!")))
```

You can see a new file jet-neko.jpg created and a new fun-looking cat, as in Figure 2-4.

Figure 2-4. *Jet cat*

Now while this setup with the auto plug-in is perfectly ok, let's see how to minimize latency between your code typing and the processing output, by using a Clojure REPL.

At the REPL

We have just reviewed how to run samples and write some Origami code in a fashion similar to the setup with Java, Scala, and Kotlin, and saw again how to include and use the auto plug-in.

Better than that, Clojure comes with a Read-Eval-Print-Loop (REPL) environment, meaning you can type in lines of code, like commands, one by one, and get them executed instantly.

To start the Clojure REPL, Leiningen has a subcommand named repl, which can be started with

```
lein repl
```

After a few startup lines are printed on the terminal/console:

```
nREPL server started on port 64044 on host 127.0.0.1 -
nrepl://127.0.0.1:64044
REPL-y 0.3.7, nREPL 0.2.11
Clojure 1.8.0
Java HotSpot(TM) 64-Bit Server VM 1.8.0_151-b12
    Docs: (doc function-name-here)
          (find-doc "part-of-name-here")
  Source: (source function-name-here)
 Javadoc: (javadoc java-object-or-class-here)
    Exit: Control+D or (exit) or (quit)
 Results: Stored in vars *1, *2, *3, an exception in *e
```

You will then be greeted with the REPL prompt:

```
opencv3.ok=>
```

opencv3.ok is the main namespace of the project, and you can type in code at the prompt just like you were typing code in the opencv3/ok.clj file. For example, let's check whether the underlying OpenCV library is loaded properly by printing its version:

```
(println "Using OpenCV Version: " opencv3.core/VERSION "..")
; Using OpenCV Version:  3.3.1-dev ..
```

The library is indeed loaded properly, and native binding is found via Leiningen's magic.

Let's use it right now for a kick-start. The following two lines get some functions from the utils namespace, mainly to open a frame, and then load an image and open it into that frame:

```
(require '[opencv3.utils :as u])
(u/show (imread "resources/minicat.jpg"))
```

The cute cat from Figure 2-5 should now be showing up on your computer as well.

Figure 2-5. *Cute cat*

Origami encourages the notion of pipelines for image manipulation. So, to read an image, convert the color of the loaded image, and show the resulting image in a frame, you would usually pipe all the function calls one after the other, using the Clojure threading macro ->, just like in the following one-liner:

```
(-> "resources/minicat.jpg" imread (cvt-color! COLOR_RGB2GRAY)
(u/show))
```

Which now converts the minicat.jpg from Figure 2-5 to its gray version as in Figure 2-6.

Figure 2-6. *Grayed cute cat*

-> does nothing more than reorganize code so that the first invocation result goes to the input of the next line and so on. This makes for very swift and compact image-processing code.

Note that the lines execute directly, so you don't have to wait for file changes or anything and can just get the result onscreen as you press the Enter key.

Instant gratification.

Instant gratification takes too long.

Carrie Fisher

REPL from Atom

The REPL started by Leiningen is quite nice, with a bunch of other features you can discover through the documentation, but it's hard to compete with the autocompletion provided by a standard text editor.

Using all the same project metadata from the **project.clj** file, the Atom editor can actually provide, via a plug-in, instant and visual completion choices.

The plug-in to install is named proto-repl. Effectively, you will need to install two plug-ins

- the ink plug-in, required by prot-repl

- the proto-repl plug-in

to get the same setup on your atom editor, as shown in Figure 2-7.

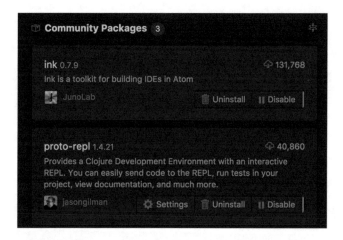

Figure 2-7. *Install two plug-ins in Atom: ink and proto-repl*

The same Leiningen-based REPL can be started either by the atom menu as in Figure 2-8 or by the equivalent key shortcut.

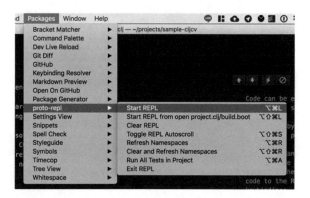

Figure 2-8. *Start a REPL from within Atom*

When starting the REPL, a window named Proto-REPL opens on the right-hand side of the Atom editor. This is exactly the same REPL that you have used when executing the **lein repl** command directly from the terminal. So, you can type in code there too.

But the real gem of this setup is to have autocompletion and choice presented to you when typing code, as in Figure 2-9.

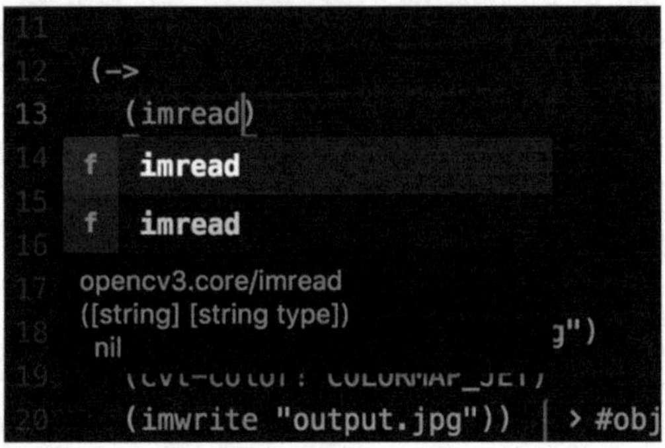

Figure 2-9. Instant completion

You can now retype the code to read and convert the color of an image directly in a file, let's say **ok.clj**. Your setup should now be similar to that shown in Figure 2-10.

Figure 2-10. *Atom editor + Clojure code*

Once you have typed the code in, you can select code and execute the selected lines of code by using Ctrl-Alt+s (on Mac, Command-Ctrl+s).

You can also execute the code block before the cursor by using Ctrl-Alt+b (on Mac, Command-Ctrl+b) and get your shot of instant gratification.

After code evaluation, and a slight tab arrangement, you can have instant code writing on the left-hand side, and the image transformation feedback on the right-hand side, just as in Figure 2-11.

Figure 2-11. *The ideal editor-based computer vision environment*

The jet-set cat is now showing in the output.jpg file, and can be updated by updating and executing code in the opened editor tab.

For example, see by yourself what happens when adding the **resize!** function call in the processing flow, as in the following code.

```
(->
    (imread "resources/cat.jpg")
    (resize! (new-size 150 100))
    (cvt-color! COLORMAP_JET)
    (imwrite "output.jpg"))
```

Nice. A newly resized jet-set cat is now instantly showing on **your** screen.

Gorilla Notebook

To complete this recipe, let's present how to use gorilla from within an Origami project.

Gorilla is a Leiningen plug-in, where you can write and run notebooks, à la python's jupyter.

This means you can write code alongside documentation, and even better, you can also share those *notes* to the outside world.

How does that work? Gorilla takes your project setup and uses it to execute the code in a background REPL. Hence, it will find the origami/opencv setup taken from the **project.clj** file.

It will also start a web server whose goal is to serve notes or worksheets. Worksheets are pages where you can write lines of code and execute them.

You can also write documentation in the sheet itself in the form of markdown markup, which renders to HTML.

As a result, each of the notes, or worksheets, ends up being effectively a miniblog.

The **project.clj** file that comes with the clj-opencv template defines a convenient leiningen alias to start gorilla via the notebook alias:

```
:aliases {"notebook" ["gorilla" ":ip" "0.0.0.0" ":port"
"10000"]}
```

This effectively tells leiningen to convert the **notebook** subcommand to the following gorilla command:

```
lein gorilla :ip 0.0.0.0 :port 10000
```

Let's try it, by using the following command on a console or terminal:

```
lein notebook
```

After a few seconds, the Gorilla REPL is started. You can access it already at the following location:

```
http://localhost:10000/worksheet.html?filename=notes/practice.clj
```

You will be presented with a worksheet like in Figure 2-12.

Figure 2-12.   *Gorilla notebook and a cat*

In a gorilla notebook, every block of the page is either Clojure code or markdown text. You can turn the currently highlighted block to text mode by using Alt+g, Alt+m (or Ctrl+g, Ctrl+m on Mac) where m is for markdown, as in Figure 2-13.

```
this is a block of **text** written in __markdown__
```

Figure 2-13.   *Markdown text mode*

You can also turn back the highlighted block into code mode by using Alt+g, Alt+j (or Ctrl+g, Ctrl+j on Mac), where j is for Clojure, as in Figure 2-14.

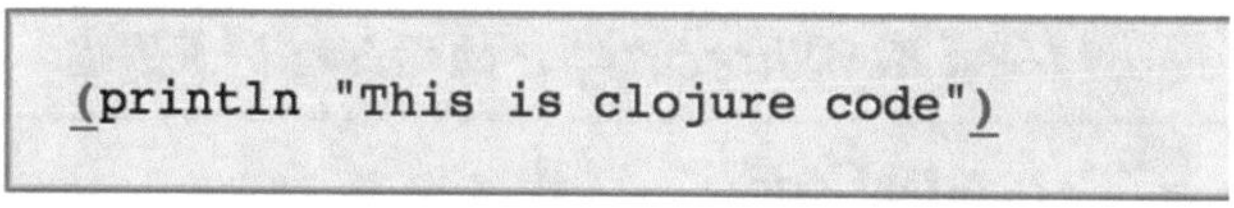

```
(println "This is clojure code")
```

Figure 2-14. *Block of code*

To execute the highlighted block of code, you would use Shift+Enter, and the block turns into executed mode, as in Figure 2-15.

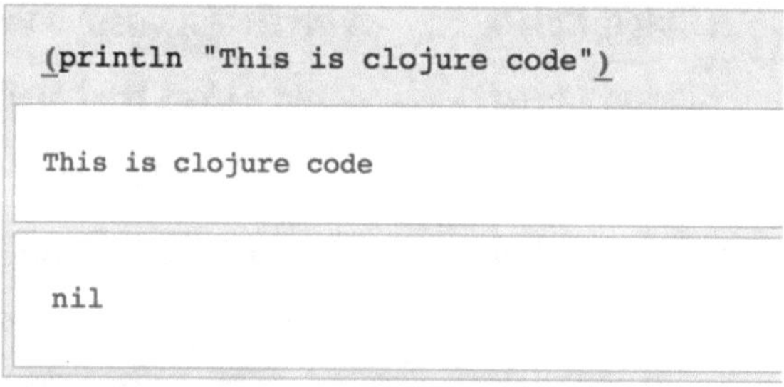

```
(println "This is clojure code")

This is clojure code


nil
```

Figure 2-15. *Clojure code was executed*

What that does is read from the code block, send the input to the background REPL via a websocket, retrieve the result, and print it the underlying div of the code block.

To make it easy to navigate a worksheet, the most used shortcuts have been gathered in Table 2-1.

Table 2-1. *Most Used Key Shorcuts for the Gorilla REPL*

Shortcut Windows/Linux	Shortcut Mac	Usage
↑	↑	Go to the block above
↓	↓	Go to the block below
Shift+Enter	Shift+Enter	Evaluate the highlighted block
Alt+g, Alt+b	Ctrl+g, Ctrl+b	Insert a block **before** the current one
Alt+g, Alt+n	Ctrl+g, Ctrl+n	Insert a block **next to** the current one
Alt+g, Alt+u	Ctrl+g, Ctrl+u	Move the current block **up** one block
Alt+g, Alt+d	Ctrl+g, Ctrl+d	Move the current block **down** one block
Alt+g, Alt+x	Ctrl+g, Ctrl+x	**Delete** the current block
Alt+space	Ctrl+space	Autocompletion options
Alt+g, Alt+s	Ctrl+g, Ctrl+s	**Save** the current worksheet
Alt+g, Alt+l	Ctrl+g, Ctrl+l	**Load** a worksheet (a file)
Alt+g, Alt+e	Ctrl+g, Ctrl+e	Save the current worksheet to a new file name

Alright; so now you know all that is needed to start typing code in the gorilla REPL. Let's try this out right now. In a new code block of the worksheet, try to type in the following Clojure code.

```
(-> "http://eskipaper.com/images/jump-cat-1.jpg"
 (u/mat-from-url)
 (u/resize-by 0.3)
 (u/mat-view))
```

And now... **Shift+Enter!** This should bring you close to Figure 2-16 and a new shot of instant gratification.

```
(-> "http://eskipaper.com/images/jump-cat-1.jpg"
    (u/mat-from-url)
    (u/resize-by 0.3)
    (u/mat-view))
```

Figure 2-16. *Instant jumping cat*

Remember that all of this is happening in the browser, which has three direct positive consequences.

The first one is that remote people can actually view your worksheets, and they can provide documentation directly from their own machines by connecting to the URL directly.

Second, they can also execute code directly block by block to understand the flow.

Third, the saved format of the worksheets is such that they can be used as standard namespaces and can be used through normal code-writing workflow. Conversely, it also means that standard Clojure files can be opened, and documentation can be added via the Gorilla REPL.

From now on, we won't impose using either the Gorilla REPL or the Atom environment, or even simply typing on the REPL. Effectively, these are three different views on the same project setup.

Simply remember for now that to show a picture, the function to use is slightly different depending on whether you are in the Gorilla REPL or in a standard REPL.

In the Gorilla REPL:

```
(u/mat-view)
```

In the standard REPL:

```
(u/show)
```

In atom, you would save the file:

```
(imwrite mat "output.jpg")
```

OK, this time you are really all set! Time for some computer vision basics.

2-2 Working with Mats

Problem

As you remember from Chapter 1, Mat is your best friend when working with OpenCV. You also remember functions like new Mat(), setTo, copyTo, and so on to manipulate Mat. Now, you wonder how you can do basic Mat operations using the Origami library.

Solution

Since Origami is mainly a wrapper around OpenCV, all the same functions are present in the API. This recipe shows basic Mat operations again, and takes them further by presenting code tricks made possible by using Clojure.

How it works

Creating a Mat

Remember that you need a height, a width, and a number of channels to create a mat. This is done using the **new-mat** function. The following snippet creates a 30×30 Mat, with one channel per pixel, each value being an integer.

```
(def mat (new-mat 30 30 CV_8UC1))
```

If you try to display the content of the mat, either with u/mat-view (gorilla repl) or u/show (standard repl), then the memory assigned to the mat is actually left as is. See Figure 2-17.

Figure 2-17. *New Mat with no assigned color*

Let's assign a color, the same to every pixel of the Mat. This is either done when creating the Mat, **or** can be done with **set-to**, which is a call to the **.setTo** Java function of OpenCV.

```
(def mat (new-mat 30 30 CV_8UC1 (new-scalar 105)))
; or
```

```
(def mat (new-mat 30 30 CV_8UC1))
(set-to mat (new-scalar 105))
```

Every pixel in the mat now has value 105 assigned to it (Figure 2-18).

Figure 2-18. *Mat with assigned color*

To understand most of the underlying matrix concepts of OpenCV, it is usually a good idea for you to check the values of the underlying mat using **.dump** or simply **dump.**

This will be done a few times in this chapter. To use it, simply call dump on the mat you want to see the internals from.

```
(->>
  (new-scalar 128.0)
  (new-mat 3 3 CV_8UC1)
  (dump))
```

And the expected output is shown in the following, with the mat points all set to the value of 128.

```
[128 128 128]
[128 128 128]
[128 128 128]
```

.dump calls the original OpenCV function and will print all the row and column pixel values in one string.

```
"[128, 128, 128;\n 128, 128, 128;\n 128, 128, 128]"
```

Creating a Colored Mat

With one channel per pixel, you can only specify the white intensity of each pixel, and thus, you can only create gray mats.

To create a colored mat, you need three channels, and by default, each channel's value representing the intensity of red, blue, and green.

To create a 30×30 red mat, the following snippet will create an empty three-channel mat with each point in the mat set to the RGB value of [255 0 0] (yes, this is inverted, so be careful):

```
(def red-mat    (new-mat 30 30 CV_8UC3 (new-scalar 0 0 255)))
```

In a similar way, to create a blue or green mat:

```
(def green-mat  (new-mat 30 30 CV_8UC3 (new-scalar 0 255 0)))
(def blue-mat   (new-mat 30 30 CV_8UC3 (new-scalar 255 0 0)))
```

If you execute all this in the gorilla REPL, each of the mats shows up, as in Figure 2-19.

Figure 2-19. *Red, green, and blue mats*

Using a Submat

You will remember that we have seen how to use a submat in Chapter 1; let's review how to use those submats using origami.

Here, we first create an RGB mat with three channels per pixel, and set all the pixels to a cyan color.

A submat can then be created using, well, the **submat** function and a rectangle to define the size of the submat.

This gives the following code snippet:

```
(def mat (new-mat 30 30 CV_8UC3 (new-scalar 255 255 0)))
(def sub (submat mat (new-rect 10 10 10 10)))
(set-to sub (new-scalar 0 255 255))
```

The resulting main mat, with yellow inside where the submat was defined, and the rest of the mat in cyan color, is shown in Figure 2-20.

Figure 2-20. *Submats with Origami*

Just for the kicks at this stage, see what a one-liner of origami code can do, by using **hconcat!**, a function that concatenates multiple mats together, and **clojure.core/repeat**, which creates a sequence of the same item.

```
(u/mat-view (hconcat! (clojure.core/repeat 10 mat3)))
```

The resulting pattern is shown in Figure 2-21.

Figure 2-21. *Origami fun*

At this point, you can already figure out some creative generative patterns by yourself.

Setting One Pixel Color

Setting all the colors of a mat was done using **set-to**. Setting one pixel to a color is done using the Java method **put**. The **put** function takes a position in the mat, and a byte array representing the RGB values of that pixel.

So, if you want to create a 3×3 mat with all its pixels to yellow, you would use the following code snippet.

```
(def yellow (byte-array [0 238 238]))

(def a (new-mat 3 3 CV_8UC3))

(.put a 0 0 yellow)
(.put a 0 1 yellow)
(.put a 0 2 yellow)

(.put a 1 0 yellow)
(.put a 1 1 yellow)
(.put a 1 2 yellow)

(.put a 2 0 yellow)
(.put a 2 1 yellow)
(.put a 2 2 yellow)
```

Unfortunately, the 3×3 mat is a bit too small for this book, so you should type in the code yourself.

The dump function works nicely here though, and you can see the content of the yellow mat in the following:

```
[0 238 238 0 238 238 0 238 238]
[0 238 238 0 238 238 0 238 238]
[0 238 238 0 238 238 0 238 238]
```

Typing all this line by line is a bit tiring though, so this where you use Clojure code to loop over the pixel as needed.

A call to Clojure core **doseq** gets convenient to reduce the boilerplate.

```
(doseq [x [0 1 2]
        y [0 1 2]]
  (prn  "x=" x "; y=" y))
```

The preceding simple doseq snippet simply loops over all the pixels of a 3×3 mat.

```
"x=" 0 "; y=" 0
"x=" 0 "; y=" 1
"x=" 0 "; y=" 2
"x=" 1 "; y=" 0
"x=" 1 "; y=" 1
...
```

So, to have a bit more fun, let's display some random red variants for each pixel of a 100×100 colored mat. This would be pretty tiresome by hand, so let's use the doseq sequence here too.

```
(def height 100)
(def width 100)

(def a (new-mat height width CV_8UC3))
(doseq [x (range width)
        y (range height)]
  (.put a x y (byte-array [0 0 (rand 255)])))
```

Figure 2-22 gives one version of the executed snippet.

Figure 2-22. *Randomly filled mat with variant of red pixels*

Piping Process and Some Generative Art

You can already see how Origami makes it quite simple and fun to integrate generative work with OpenCV mats.

This short section will also be a quick introduction to the piping process that is encouraged by Origami.

Clojure has two main constructs (called macros) named -> and ->>. They **pipe** results throughout consecutive function calls.

The result of the first function call is passed as a parameter to the second function, and then the result of that call to the second function is passed on the third one, and so on.

The first macro, ->, passes the result as the first parameter to the next function call.

The second macro, ->>, passes the result as the last parameter to the next function call.

For example, creating a random gray mat could be done this way:

```
(->> (rand 255)
     (double)
     (new-scalar)
     (new-mat 30 30 CV_8UC1)
     (u/mat-view))
```

Which, read line by line, gives the following steps:

- A random value is generated with rand; that value is between 0 and 255.

- The generated value is a float, so we turn the value to double.

- new-scalar is used to create the equivalent of a byte array that OpenCV can conveniently handle.

- We then create a new 30×30 mat of one channel and pass the scalar to the new-mat function to set the color of the mat to the randomly generated value.

- Finally, we can view the generated mat (Figure 2-23).

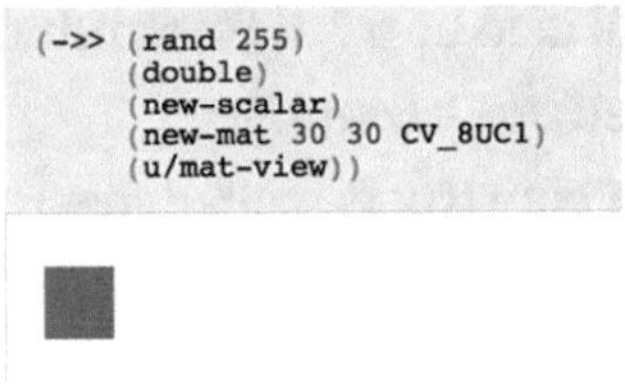

```
(->> (rand 255)
     (double)
     (new-scalar)
     (new-mat 30 30 CV_8UC1)
     (u/mat-view))
```

Figure 2-23. *Generated random gray mat*

You could do the same with a randomly colored mat as well. This time, the rand function is called three times (Figure 2-24).

```
(->> (new-scalar (rand 255) (rand 255) (rand 255))
     (new-mat 30 30 CV_8UC3)
     (u/mat-view))
```

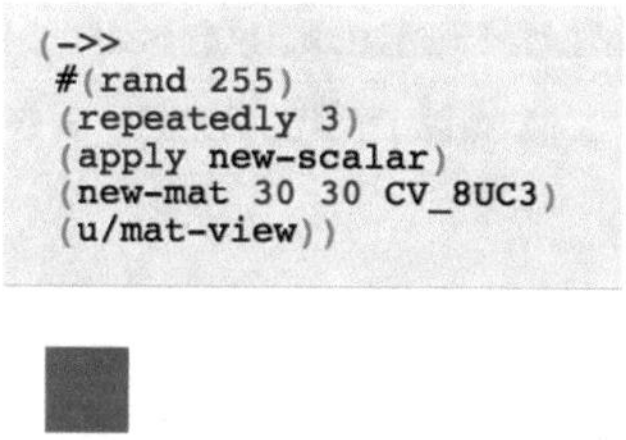

```
(->>
 #(rand 255)
 (repeatedly 3)
 (apply new-scalar)
 (new-mat 30 30 CV_8UC3)
 (u/mat-view))
```

Figure 2-24.

Or, with the same result, but using a few more Clojure core functions:

```
(->>
 #(rand 255)
 (repeatedly 3)
 (apply new-scalar)
 (new-mat 30 30 CV_8UC3)
 (u/mat-view))
```

where

- # creates an anonymous function

- repeatedly calls the preceding function three times to generate an array of three random values

- apply uses the array as parameters to new-scalar

- new-mat, as you have seen before, creates a mat

- u/mat-view displays the mat (Figure 2-24) in the gorilla REPL

You can see now how you could also build on those mini code flows to build different generative variations of mat. You can also combine those mats, of course, using **hconcat!** or **vconcat!** functions of OpenCV.

The following new snippet generates a sequence of 25 elements using range and then creates gray mats in the range of 0–255 by scaling the range values (Figure 2-25).

```
(->> (range 25)
    (map #(new-mat 30 30 CV_8UC1 (new-scalar (double (* % 10)))))
    (hconcat!)
    (u/mat-view))
```

Figure 2-25. *A gray gradient of 25 mats*

You can also smooth things up by generating a range of 255 values, and making the created mat slightly smaller, with each mat of size 2×10 (Figure 2-26).

```
(->> (range 255)
    (map #(new-mat 20 2 CV_8UC1 (new-scalar (double %))))
    (hconcat!)
    (u/mat-view))
```

Figure 2-26. *Smooth gray gradient of 255 mats*

2-3 Loading, Showing, Saving Mats

Problem

You have seen how to create and generate mats; now you would like to save them, reopen them, and open mats located in a URL.

Solution

Origami wraps the two main opencv functions to interact with the filesystem, namely, imread and imwrite.

It also presents a new function called imshow that you may have seen before if you have used standard opencv before. It will be covered in greater detail here.

Finally, u/mat-from-url is an origami utility function that allows you to retrieve a mat that is hosted on the net.

How it works

Loading

imread works the exact same as its opencv equivalent; this mostly means that you simply give it a path from the filesystem, and the file is read and converted to a ready-to-be-used Mat object.

In its simplest form, loading an image can be done as in the following short code snippet:

```
(def mat (imread "resources/kitten.jpg"))
```

The file path, **resources/kitten.jpg**, is relative to the project, or can also be a full path on the file system.

The resulting loaded Mat object is shown in Figure 2-27.

Figure 2-27. *"This is not a cat."*

Following the opencv documentation, the following image file formats are currently supported by Origami:

- Windows bitmaps - `*.bmp, *.dib`

- JPEG files - `*.jpeg, *.jpg, *.jpe`

- Portable Network Graphics - `*.png`

- Sun rasters - `*.sr, *.ras`

The following are also usually supported by OpenCV but may not be supported on all platforms coming with Origami:

- JPEG 2000 files - `*.jp2`

- WebP - `*.webp`

- Portable image format - `*.pbm, *.pgm, *.ppm`

- TIFF files - `*.tiff, *.tif`

When loading an image, you can refer to Table 1-3 to specify the option used to load the image, such as grayscale, and resize at the same time.

To load in grayscale and resize the image to a quarter of its size, you could use the following snippet, written using the pipeline style you have just seen.

```
(-> "resources/kitten.jpg"
    (imread IMREAD_REDUCED_GRAYSCALE_4)
    (u/mat-view))
```

It loads the same picture, but the mat looks different this time, as its color has been converted, like in Figure 2-28.

Figure 2-28. *"This is not a gray cat."*

Saving

The imwrite function from Origami takes from opencv's imwrite, but reverses the order of the parameters to make the function easy to use in processing pipes.

For example, to write the previously loaded gray cat to a new file, you would use

```
(imwrite mat "grey-neko.png")
```

A new file, **grey-neko.png**, will be created from the loaded mat object (Figure 2-29).

Figure 2-29. *grey-neko.png*

You can observe that the resulting file image has actually been converted from jpg to png for you, just by specifying it as the extension in the file name.

The reason that the parameter order has been changed is that, in this case, you can save images from within the pipeline code flow.

See in the following how the image is saved during the flow of transformation.

```
(-> "resources/kitten.jpg"
    (imread IMREAD_REDUCED_GRAYSCALE_4)
    (imwrite "grey-neko.png")
    (u/mat-view))
```

The mat will be saved in the file image grey-neko.png, and the processing will go on to the next step, here mat-view.

Showing

Origami comes with a quick way of previewing images, and streams in the form of the **imshow** function, from the opencv3.utils namespace.

```
(-> "resources/kitten.jpg"
    (imread)
    (u/imshow))
```

The **imshow** function takes a mat as the parameter and opens a Java frame with the mat inside, as shown in Figure 2-30.

Figure 2-30. *Framed cat*

The frame opened by **imshow** has a few default sets of key shortcuts, as shown in Table 2-2.

Table 2-2. *Default Keys in Quick View*

Key	Action
Q	Close Frame
F	Full Screen Frame; press again to return to window mode
S	Quick Save the picture currently showing

This is not all; you can pass a map when using **imshow** to define various settings from the background color of the frame to its size and so forth. Also, a handlers section can be added to the map, where you can define your own key shortcuts.

See an example of the configuration map for the following frame.

```
{:frame
  {:color "#000000" :title "image" :width 400 :height 400}
  :handlers
  { 85 #(gamma! % 0.1) 86 #(gamma! % -0.1)}}
```

In the **handlers** section, each entry of the map is made of an ASCII key code and a function. The function takes a mat and has to return a mat. Here, you can suppose gamma! is a function changing brightness on a mat, depending on a brightness parameter.

Figure 2-31 shows the mat after pressing u.

Figure 2-31. *Dark cat*

Figure 2-32 shows the mat after pressing v.

Figure 2-32. *Bright cat*

This is not the most important section of this book, but the quick frame becomes quite handy when playing with the video streams later on in Chapter 4.

Loading from URL

While it is usually the case that the picture can be accessed from the filesystem the code is running on, many times there is a need to process a picture that is remotely hosted.

Origami provides a basic **mat-from-url** function that takes a URL and turns it into an OpenCV mat.

The standard way to do this in origami is shown in the following snippet:

```
(-> "http://www.hellonico.info/static/cat-peekaboo.jpg"
  (u/mat-from-url)
  (u/mat-view))
```

And the resulting image is shown in Figure 2-33.

Figure 2-33.   *Cat from the Internet*

This was the only way to load a picture until recently. But then, most of the time, you would be doing something like

```
(-> "http://www.hellonico.info/static/cat-peekaboo.jpg"
  (u/mat-from-url)
  (u/resize-by 0.5)
  (u/mat-view))
```

to resize the picture right after loading it. Now, u/mat-from-url also accepts imread parameters. So, to load the remote picture in gray, and reduce its size altogether, you can directly pass in the IMREAD_* parameter. Note that this has the side effect of creating a temporary file on the filesystem.

```
(-> "http://www.hellonico.info/static/cat-peekaboo.jpg"
    (u/mat-from-url IMREAD_REDUCED_GRAYSCALE_4)
    (u/mat-view))
```

The same remote picture is now both smaller and loaded in black and white, as shown in Figure 2-34.

Figure 2-34. *Return of the cat in black and white*

2-4 Working with Colors, ColorMaps, and ColorSpaces

Color is the place where our brain and the universe meet.

Paul Klee

Problem

You want to learn a bit more about how to handle colors in OpenCV. Up to now, we have only seen colors using the RGB encoding. There must be some more!

Solution

Origami provides two simple namespaces, opencv3.colors.html and opencv3.colors.rgb, to create the scalar values used for basic coloring, so we will start by reviewing how to use those two namespaces to set colors to mat.

A color map works like a color filter, where you make the mat redder or bluer, depending on your mood.

apply-color-map! and **transform!** are the two opencv core functions used to achieve the color switch.

Finally, cvt-color! is another core opencv function that brings a mat from one color space to another one, for example from RGB to black and white. This is an important key feature of OpenCV, as most recognition algorithms cannot be used properly in standard RGB.

How it works

Simple Colors

Colors from the origami packages need to be required, and so when you use them, you need to update your namespace declaration at the top of the notebook.

```
(ns joyful-leaves
   (:require
    [opencv3.utils :as u]
    [opencv3.colors.html :as html]
    [opencv3.colors.rgb :as rgb]
    [opencv3.core :refer :all]))
```

With the namespace rgb, you can create scalars for RGB values instead of guessing them.

So, if you want to use a red color, you can get your environment to help you find and autocomplete the scalar you are looking for, as shown in Figure 2-35.

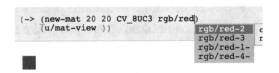

Figure 2-35. *RGB colors*

And so, using this in action, you can indeed use the following snippet to create a 20×20 mat of a red color.

```
(-> (new-mat 20 20 CV_8UC3 rgb/red-2)
    (u/mat-view ))
```

Note that since rgb/red-2 is a scalar, you can dump the values for each channel by just printing it:

```
#object[org.opencv.core.Scalar 0x4e73ed0 "[0.0, 0.0, 205.0, 0.0]"]
```

This is pretty nice to find color codes quickly.

The **opencv3.colors.html** namespace was created so that you could also use the traditional hexadecimal notation used in css. For a nice light green with a bit of blue, you could use this:

```
(html/->scalar "#66cc77")
```

In full sample mode, and using threading ->>, this gives

```
(->> (html/->scalar "#66cc77")
     (new-mat 20 20 CV_8UC3 )
     (u/mat-view ))
```

which creates a small mat of a light green/blue color (Figure 2-36).

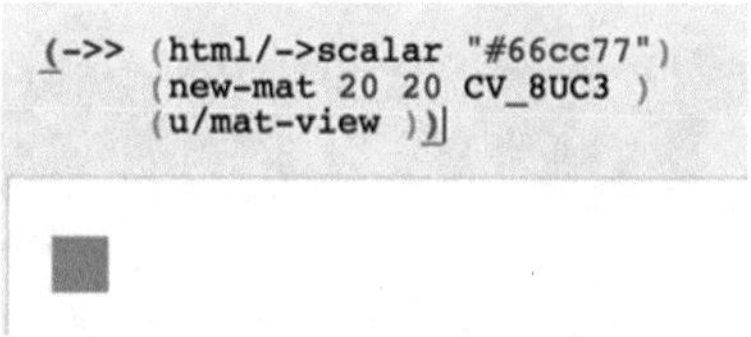

```
(->> (html/->scalar "#66cc77")
     (new-mat 20 20 CV_8UC3 )
     (u/mat-view ))]
```

Figure 2-36. *Colors using HTML codes*

Printing the color itself gives you the assigned RGB values:

```
(html/->scalar "#66cc77")
; "[119.0, 204.0, 102.0, 0.0]"
```

And you can indeed check that the colors match by creating the RGB scalar yourself.

```
(->> (new-scalar 119 204 102)
     (new-mat 20 20 CV_8UC3 ))
```

This will give you a mat with the exact same RGB-based color.

Color Maps

Color maps can be understood by a simple color change, using a simple filter, which results in something similar to your favorite smartphone photo application.

There are a few default maps that can be used with OpenCV; let's try one of them, say COLORMAP_AUTUMN, which turns the mat into a quite autumnal red.

To apply the map to a Mat, for example the cat from Figure 2-37, simply use the apply-color-map! function.

Figure 2-37. *Cat to be colored*

The following snippet shows how to make use of the usual imread and the apply-color-map sequentially.

```
(-> "resources/cat-on-sofa.jpg"
    (imread IMREAD_REDUCED_COLOR_4)
    (apply-color-map! COLORMAP_AUTUMN)
    (u/mat-view))
```

The resulting cat is shown in Figure 2-38.

Figure 2-38. *Autumn cat*

Here is the full list of standard color maps available straight out of the box; try them out!

- COLORMAP_HOT
- COLORMAP_HSV
- COLORMAP_JET
- COLORMAP_BONE
- COLORMAP_COOL
- COLORMAP_PINK
- COLORMAP_RAINBOW
- COLORMAP_OCEAN
- COLORMAP_WINTER
- COLORMAP_SUMMER
- COLORMAP_AUTUMN
- COLORMAP_SPRING

You can also define your own color space conversion. This is done by a matrix multiplication, which sounds geeky, but is actually simpler than it sounds.

We will take the example of rgb/yellow-2. You may not remember, so if you print it, you'll find out that this is actually coded as, no blue, some green, and some red, which translated into RGB gives the following: [0 238 238].

Then, we define a transformation matrix made of three columns and three rows; since we are working with RGB mats, we will do this in three-channel mode.

```
[0 0 0]      ; blue
[0 0.5 0]    ; green
[0 1 0.5]    ; red
```

What does this matrix do? Remember that we want to apply a color transformation for each pixel, meaning in output we want a set of RGB values for each pixel.

For any given pixel, the new RGB values are such that

- Blue is 0 × Input Blue + 0 × Input Green + 0 × Input Red

- Green is 0 × Input Blue + 0.5 × Input Green + 0 × Input Red

- Red is 0 × Input Blue + 1 × Input Green + 0.5 Input Red

And so, since our Mat is all yellow, we have the following input:

```
[0 238 238]
```

And the output of each pixel is such as follows:

```
[0x0 + 0x238 + 0x238, 0x0 + 0.5x238 + 0 x 238, 0x0 + 1x238 +
0.5x238]
```

Or, since 255 is the maximum value for a channel:

```
[0 119 255]
```

Now in origami code, this gives the following:

```
(def custom
  (u/matrix-to-mat [
  [0 0 0]          ; blue
  [0 0.5 0]        ; green
  [0 1 0.5]        ; red
  ]))

(-> (new-mat 3 3 CV_8UC3 rgb/yellow-2)
    (dump))
```

Here, the mat content is shown with dump:

```
[0 238 238 0 238 238 0 238 238]
[0 238 238 0 238 238 0 238 238]
[0 238 238 0 238 238 0 238 238]
```

Then:

```
(-> (new-mat 30 30 CV_8UC3 rgb/yellow-2) u/mat-view)
```

```
(-> (new-mat 3 3 CV_8UC3 rgb/yellow-2)
    (transform! custom)
    (dump))
```

And the result of the transformation is shown in the following, as expected consists of a matrix of [0 119 255] values.

```
[0 119 255 0 119 255 0 119 255]
[0 119 255 0 119 255 0 119 255]
[0 119 255 0 119 255 0 119 255]
```

```
(-> (new-mat 30 30 CV_8UC3 rgb/yellow-2)
    (transform! custom)
    u/mat-view)
```

Make sure you execute the statements one by one to see the different RGB values in the output, along with the colored mats.

You may look around in the literature, but a nice sepia transformation would use the following matrix:

```
(def sepia-2 (u/matrix-to-mat [
  [0.131 0.534 0.272]
  [0.168 0.686 0.349]
  [0.189 0.769 0.393]]))
```

```
(-> "resources/cat-on-sofa.jpg"
   (imread IMREAD_REDUCED_COLOR_4)
   (transform! sepia-2)
(u/mat-view ))
```

With the resulting sepia cat in Figure 2-39.

Figure 2-39. *Sepia cat*

Time to go out and make your own filters!

We have seen how transform is applied to each pixel in RGB. Later on, when switching to other colorspaces, you can also remember that even though the values won't be red, blue, green anymore, this **transform!** function can still be used in the same way.

Color Space

You have been working almost uniquely in the RGB color space up to now, which is the simplest one to use. In most computing cases, RGB is not the most efficient, so many other color spaces have been created in the past and are available for use. With Origami, to switch from one to the other, you usually use the function cvt-color!

What does a color space switch do?

It basically means that the three-channel values for each pixel have different meanings.

For example, red in RGB can be encoded in RGB as 0 0 238 (and its graphical representation is shown in Figure 2-40):

```
(-> (new-mat 1 1 CV_8UC3 rgb/red-2)
    (.dump))
; "[  0,    0, 238]"

(-> (new-mat 30 30 CV_8UC3 rgb/red-2)
    (u/mat-view))
```

"[0,   0, 238]"

Figure 2-40. *Red in RGB color space*

However, when you change the color space and convert it to another namespace, say HSV, Hue-Saturation-Value, the values of the matrix are changed.

```
(-> (new-mat 1 1 CV_8UC3 rgb/red-2)
    (cvt-color! COLOR_RGB2HSV)
    (.dump))

(-> (new-mat 30 30 CV_8UC3 rgb/red-2)
    (cvt-color! COLOR_RGB2HSV)
    (u/mat-view))
```

And of course, the simple display of the mat content is not really relevant anymore; as shown in Figure 2-41, it turned to yellow!!

"[120, 255, 238]"

Figure 2-41. *Red in HSV color space*

Changing color space does not mean changing anything to the colors of the mat, but changing the way those are represented internally.

Why would you want to change colorspace?

While each colorspace has its own advantages, color space HSV is widely used due to the fact that it is easy to use ranges to identify and find shapes of a given color in a mat.

In RGB, as you remember, each value of each channel represents the intensity of red, green, or blue.

In opencv cv terms, let's say we want to see a linear progression of red; we can increase or decrease the value of the two other channels, green and blue.

```
(->> (range 255)
    (map #(new-mat 20 1 CV_8UC3 (new-scalar % % 255)))
    (hconcat!)
    (u/mat-view))
```

That shows the line of Figure 2-42.

Figure 2-42.   *Linear intensity of red in RGB*

But what if in a picture, we are trying to look for orange-looking shapes? Hmm... How does that orange color look in RGB again?

Yes, it starts to get slightly difficult. Let's take a different approach and look into the HSV color space.

134

As mentioned, HSV stands for Hue-Saturation-Value:

- Hue is the color as you would understand it: it is usually a value between 0 and 360, for 360 degrees, even though OpenCV eight-bit pictures, the ones we use the most, actually use a range between 0 and 180, or half.

- Saturation is the amount of gray, and it ranges between 0 and 255.

- Value stands for brightness, and it ranges between 0 and 255.

In that case, let's see what happens if we draw this ourselves, with what we have learned so far.

The function **hsv-mat** creates a mat from a hue value.

As you can read, the code switches the color space of the mat twice, once to set the color space to HSV and set the hue, and then back to RGB so we can draw it later with the usual function **imshow** or **mat-view**.

```
(defn hsv-mat [h]
  (let[m (new-mat 20 3 CV_8UC3)]
    (cvt-color! m COLOR_BGR2HSV)
    (set-to m (new-scalar h 255 255))
    (cvt-color! m COLOR_HSV2BGR)
    m))
```

We have seen the hue ranges from 0 to 180 in OpenCV, so let's do a range on it and create a concatenated mat of all the small mats with **hconcat**.

```
(->> (range 180)
     (map hsv-mat)
     (hconcat!)
     (u/mat-view))
```

The drawn result is shown in Figure 2-43.

```
#'joyful-leaves/text-mat
```

```
0     18    36    54    72    90    108   126   144   162   180
```

```
#'joyful-leaves/hsv-mat
```

Figure 2-43. *Hue values*

First, you may notice that toward the end of the bar, the color goes back to red again. It is often considered a cylinder for that reason.

The second thing you may notice is that it is easier to just tell which color you are looking for by providing a range. 20-25 is usually used for yellow, for example.

Because it can be annoying to select red in one range, you can sometimes use the reverse RGB during the color conversion: instead of using COLOR_BGR2HSV, you can try to use COLOR_RGB2HSV (Figure 2-44).

```
#'joyful-leaves/text-mat
```

```
0     18    36    54    72    90    108   126   144   162   180
```

```
#'joyful-leaves/hsv-mat
```

Figure 2-44. *Inverted hue spectrum*

This makes it easier to select red colors, with a hue range between 105 and 150.

Let's try that on a red cat. It is hard to find a red cat in nature, so we will use a picture instead.

The cat is loaded with the following snippet (Figure 2-45).

```
(-> "resources/redcat.jpg"
    (imread IMREAD_REDUCED_COLOR_2)
    (u/mat-view))
```

Figure 2-45. *Natural red cat*

Then, we define a range of lower red and upper red. The remaining
saturation and value are set to 30 30 (sometimes 50 50) and 255 255
(sometimes 250 250), so from very dark and grayed to full-blown hue color.

```
(def lower-red  (new-scalar 105 30 30))
(def upper-red  (new-scalar 150 255 255))
```

Now, we use the opencv in-range function, which we will see again
later in recipe 2-7, to say we want to find colors in a specified range and
store the result in a mask, which is initialized as an empty mat.

```
(def mask (new-mat))
```

```
(-> "resources/redcat.jpg"
    (imread IMREAD_REDUCED_COLOR_2)
    (cvt-color! COLOR_RGB2HSV)
    (in-range lower-red upper-red mask))
```

```
(u/mat-view mask)
```

Et voila: the resulting mask mat is in Figure 2-46.

Figure 2-46. *Mask of the red colors from the picture*

We will see that finding-color technique in more detail later, but now you see why you would want to switch color space from RGB to something that is easier to work with, here again HSV.

2-5 Rotating and Transforming Mats

I shall now recall to mind that the motion of the heavenly bodies is circular, since the motion appropriate to a sphere is rotation in a circle.

Nicolaus Copernicus

Problem

You would like to start rotating mats and applying simple linear transformations.

Solution

There are three ways of achieving rotation in OpenCV.

In very simple cases, you can simply use flip, which will flip the picture horizontally, vertically, or both.

Another way is to use the rotate function, which is a simple function basically taking only an orientation constant and rotating the mat according to that constant.

The all-star way is to use the function warp-affine. More can be done with it, but it is slightly harder to master, making use of matrix computation to perform the transformation.

Let's see how all this works!

How it works

We will make use of a base image throughout this tutorial, so let's start by loading it now for further reference (Figure 2-47). And of course, yes, you can already load your own at this stage.

```
(def neko (imread "resources/ai3.jpg" IMREAD_REDUCED_COLOR_8))
(u/mat-view neko)
```

Figure 2-47. *Kitten ready for flipping and rotation*

Flipping

Alright; this one is rather easy. You just need to call flip on the image with a parameter telling how you want the flip to be done.

Note here the first-time usage of **clone** in the image-processing flow.

While flip! does transformation in place, thus modifying the picture that it is passed, clone creates a new mat, so that the original neko is left untouched.

```
(-> neko
    (clone)
    (flip! 0)
    (u/mat-view))
```

And the result is shown in Figure 2-48.

Figure 2-48. *Flipped Neko*

Most of the Origami functions work like this. The standard version, here flip, needs an input mat and an output mat, while flip! does the conversion in place and only needs an input/output mat. Also, while flip has no return value, flip! returns the output mat so it can be used in a pipeline.

Similarly, you have already seen cvt-color, and cvt-color!, or hconcat and hconcat!, and so on.

Let's play a bit with Clojure and use a sequence to show all the possible flips on a mat.

```
(->> [1 -1 0]
    (map #(-> neko clone (flip! %)))
    (hconcat!)
    (u/mat-view))
```

This time, all the flips are showing (Figure 2-49).

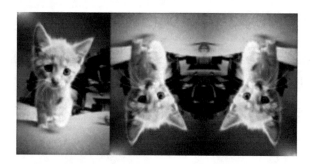

Figure 2-49. *Flip-flop*

Rotation

The function **rotate!** also takes a rotation parameter and turns the image according to it.

```
(-> neko
    (clone)
    (rotate! ROTATE_90_CLOCKWISE)
    (u/mat-view))
```

Note again the use of clone to create an intermediate mat in the processing flow, and the result in Figure 2-50.

Figure 2-50. *Clockwise-rotated cat*

Note also how clone and ->> can be used to create multiple mats from a single source.

```
(->> [ROTATE_90_COUNTERCLOCKWISE ROTATE_90_CLOCKWISE]
    (map #(-> neko clone (rotate! %)))
    (hconcat!)
    (u/mat-view))
```

In the final step, the multiple mats are concatenated using **hconcat!** (Figure 2-51) or **vconcat!** (Figure 2-52).

Figure 2-51. *Using hconcat! on rotated mats*

Figure 2-52. _Using vconcat! on rotated mats_

Thanks to the usage of clone, the original mat is left untouched and can still be used in other processing pipelines as if it had just been freshly loaded.

Warp

The last one, as promised, is the slightly more complicated version of rotating a picture using the opencv function **warp-affine** along with a rotation matrix.

The rotation matrix is created using the function get-rotation-matrix-2-d and three parameters:

- a rotation point,

- a rotation angle,

- a zoom value.

In this first example, we keep the zoom factor to 1 and take a rotation angle of 45 degrees.

We also make the rotation point the center of the original mat.

```
(def img (clone neko))

(def rotation-angle 45)
(def zoom 1)

(def matrix
  (get-rotation-matrix-2-d
    (new-point (/ (.width img) 2) (/ (.height img) 2))
    rotation-angle
    zoom))
```

matrix is also a 2×3 Mat, made of Float values, as you can see if you print it out. The rotation matrix can then be passed to the warp function. Warp also takes a size to create the resulting mat with the proper dimension.

```
(warp-affine! img matrix (.size img))
(u/mat-view img)
```

And the 45-degrees-rotated cat is shown in Figure 2-53.

Figure 2-53.   *45 degrees*

Let's now push the fun a bit more with some autogeneration techniques. Let's create a mat that is made of the concatenation of multiple mats of rotated cats, each cat rotated with a different rotation factor.

For this purpose, let's create a function **rotate-by!,** which takes an image and an angle and applies the rotation internally, using get-rotation-matrix-2-d.

```
(defn rotate-by! [img angle]
  (let [M2
    (get-rotation-matrix-2-d
    (new-point (/ (.width img) 2) (/ (.height img) 2)) angle 1)]
    (warp-affine! img M2 (.size img))))
```

Then you can use that function in a small pipeline. The pipeline takes a range of rotations between 0 and 360, and applies each angle in sequence to the original neko mat.

```
(->> (range 0 360 40)
     (map #(-> neko clone (rotate-by! % )))
     (hconcat!)
     (u/mat-view))
```

And the fun concatenated mats are shown in Figure 2-54.

Figure 2-54. *Range and rotation*

Furthermore, let's enhance the rotate-by! function to also use an optional zoom parameter. If the zoom factor is not specified, its value defaults to 1.

```
(defn rotate-by!
  ([img angle] (rotate-by! img angle 1))
  ([img angle zoom]
```

```
(let
  [M2
    (get-rotation-matrix-2-d
        (new-point (/ (.width img) 2) (/ (.height img) 2))
angle zoom)]
  (warp-affine! img M2 (.size img)))))
```

The zoom parameter is then passed to the get-rotation-matrix-2-d function.

This time, the snippet simply does a range over seven random zoom values.

```
(->> (range 7)
    (map (fn[_] (-> neko clone (rotate-by! 0 (rand 5)))))
    (hconcat!)
    (u/mat-view))
```

And the result is shown in Figure 2-55. Also note that when the zoom value is too small, default black borders can be seen in the resulting small mat.

Figure 2-55. *Seven randomly zoomed cats*

In the same way, many other image transformations can be done with warp-affine, by passing matrixes created with a transformation matrix using get-affine-transform, get-perspective-transform, and so forth.

Most of the transformations take a source matrix of points and a target matrix of points, and each of the opencv get-** functions creates a transformation matrix to accordingly map from one set of points to the others.

When OpenCV requires a mat of "something," you can use the origami constructors, matrix-to-matofxxx from the util package.

```
(def src
  (u/matrix-to-matofpoint2f [[0 0]
                             [5 5]
                             [4 6]]))
(def dst
  (u/matrix-to-matofpoint2f [[2 0]
                             [5 5]
                             [4 6]]))
(def transform-mat (get-affine-transform src dst))
```

Applying the transformation is done in the same way with warp-affine.

```
(-> neko clone (warp-affine! transform-mat (.size neko)) u/mat-
view)
```

Figure 2-56 shows the result of the affine transformation.

Figure 2-56. *Feline affine transformation*

2-6 Filtering Mats

Problem

In contrast to mat transformations, where shapes are distorted and points are moved, filtering applies an operation to each pixel of the original mat.

This recipe is about getting to know the different filtering methods available.

Solution

In this recipe, we will first look at how to create and apply a manual filter by manually changing the values of each pixel in the mat.

Since this is boring, we will then move on to using **multiply!** to efficiently change the colors and luminosity of the mat by applying a coefficient of each channel value.

Next, we will move to some experiments with **filter-2-d,** which is used to apply a custom-made filter to the mat.

The recipe will finish with examples of how to use **threshold** and **adaptive-threshold** to keep only part of the information in a mat.

How it works

Manual Filter

The first example is a function that sets all but one of a channel's values to 0, in a three-channel picture. That has the effect of completely changing the color of the mat.

Notice how the function internally creates a fully sequential byte array of all the bytes of the mat. 3 is used here because we are supposing that we are working with a mat made of three channels per pixel.

```
(defn filter-buffer! [image _mod]
  (let [ total (* 3 (.total image))
         bytes (byte-array total)]
        (.get image 0 0 bytes)
        (doseq [^int i (range 0 total)]
        (if (not (= 0 (mod (+ i _mod) 3)))
          (aset-byte bytes i 0)))
        (.put image 0 0 bytes)
        image))
```

The mod if statement makes it so we set all values of that channel to 0 for all pixels in the mat.

We then use a new cat picture (Figure 2-57).

Figure 2-57. *Beautiful French cat*

And simply put our function into action. The value 0 in the parameter means that all but the blue channel will be set to 0.

```
(->
  "resources/emilie1.jpg"
  (imread)
  (filter-buffer! 0)
  (u/mat-view))
```

And yes, the resulting picture is overly blue (Figure 2-58).

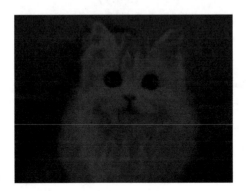

Figure 2-58. *Blue cat*

Playing with Clojure code generative capability here again, we range over the channels to create a concatenated mat of all three mats (Figure 2-59).

```
(def source
    (imread "resources/emilie1.jpg"))

(->> (range 0 3)
    (map #(filter-buffer! (clone source) %))
    (hconcat!)
    (u/mat-view))
```

Figure 2-59. *Three cats*

Multiply

It was nice to create a filter manually to see the details of how its filters are working, but actually, OpenCV has a function called **multiply** that does exactly all of this already for you.

The function takes a mat, created with origami's matrix-to-mat-of-double, to apply a multiplication to the value of each channel in a pixel.

So, in an RGB-encoded picture, using matrix [1.0 0.5 0.0] means that

- the blue channel will stay as is; the blue channel value will be multiplied by 1.0

- the green channel value will be halved; its values will be multiplied by 0.5

- The red channel value will be set to 0; its values will be multiplied by 0.

Putting this straight into action, we use the following short snippet to turn the white cat into a mellow blue picture (Figure 2-60).

```
(->
  "resources/emilie1.jpg"
  (imread)
  (multiply! (u/matrix-to-mat-of-double [ [1.0 0.5 0.0]] ))
  (u/mat-view))
```

Figure 2-60. *Mellow cat*

Luminosity

Combined with what you have learned already in chapter 2 about changing the channels, you may remember that while RGB is great at changing the intensity of a specific color channel, changing the luminosity value can be easily done in the HSV color space.

Here again, we use the multiply function of OpenCV, but this time, the color space of the mat is changed to HSV ahead of the multiplication.

```
(->
  "resources/emilie1.jpg"
  (imread)
  (cvt-color! COLOR_BGR2HSV)
  (multiply! (u/matrix-to-mat-of-double [ [1.0 1.0 1.5]] ))
  (cvt-color! COLOR_HSV2RGB)
(u/mat-view))
```

Note how the matrix used with multiply only applies a 1.5 factor to the third channel of each pixel, which in the HSV color space is indeed the luminosity. A bright result is shown in Figure 2-61.

Figure 2-61. *Bright cat*

Highlight

The preceding short snippet actually gives you a nice way of highlighting an element in a mat. Say you create a submat, or you have access to it through some finding shape algorithm; you can apply the luminosity effect to highlight only that part of the whole mat.

This is what the following new snippet does:

- It loads the main mat into the img variable

- It creates a processing pipeline focusing on a submat of img

- The color conversion and the multiply operation are done only on the submat

```
(def img (->
  "resources/emilie1.jpg"
  (imread)))

(-> img
  (submat (new-rect 100 50 100 100))
  (cvt-color! COLOR_RGB2HLS)
  (multiply! (u/matrix-to-mat-of-double [ [1.0 1.3 1.3]] ))
  (cvt-color! COLOR_HLS2RGB))

(u/mat-view img)
```

The resulting highlight mat is shown in Figure 2-62.

Figure 2-62. *Cat face*

Filter 2d

filter-2-d, the new OpenCV function introduced here, also performs operations on bytes. But this time, it computes the value of each pixel of the target mat, depending on the value of the src pixel and the values of the surrounding pixel.

To understand how it is possible to do absolutely nothing, let's take an example where the multiplication keeps the value of the pixel as is, by applying a filter that multiplies the value of current's pixel by 1, and ignoring the values of its neighbors. For this effect, the 3×3 filter matrix has a value of 1 in the center (the target pixel) and 0 for all the other ones, the surrounding neighbor pixels.

```
(-> "resources/emilie4.jpg"
    (imread)
    (filter-2-d! -1 (u/matrix-to-mat
      [[0 0 0]
       [0 1 0]
       [0 0 0]]))
    (u/mat-view))
```

This does nothing! Great. We all want more of that. The filter-2-d function call really just keeps the image as is, as shown in Figure 2-63.

Figure 2-63. *Undisturbed cat*

Let's get back to matrixes and raw pixel values to understand a bit more about how things work under the hood, with an example using a simple gray matrix.

```
(def m (new-mat 100 100 CV_8UC1 (new-scalar 200.0)))
```

The preceding snippet, as you know by now, creates a small 100×100 gray mat (Figure 2-64).

Figure 2-64. *Gray mat*

Now, we'll focus on a portion of that gray mat using submat and apply the filter-2-d function only on the submat.

We take a 3×3 matrix for the operation and use a 0.3 value for the main center pixel. This means that when we apply the filter, the value of the corresponding pixel in the target matrix will be 200×0.25=50.

```
(def s (submat m (new-rect 10 10 50 50)))
(filter-2-d! s -1
    (u/matrix-to-mat
      [[0 0 0]
       [0 0.25 0]
       [0 0 0]]))
```

Here, that means the entire submat will be darker than the pixels not located in the submat, as confirmed in Figure 2-65.

Figure 2-65. *Submat has changed*

And if you look at the pixel values themselves on a much smaller mat, you'll see that the value of the center pixel (the submat) has been divided by exactly 4.

```
(def m (new-mat 3 3 CV_8UC1 (new-scalar 200.0)))
(def s (submat m (new-rect 1 1 1 1)))
(filter-2-d! s -1 (u/matrix-to-mat
      [[0 0 0]
       [0 0.25 0]
       [0 0 0]]))
(dump m)
```

```
;  [200 200 200]
;  [200  50 200]
;  [200 200 200]
```

What else can you do with filter-2-d? It can be used for art effects as well; you can create your own filters with your custom values. So, go ahead and experiment.

```
(-> "resources/emilie4.jpg"
    (imread)
    (filter-2-d! -1 (u/matrix-to-mat
     [[17.8824     -43.5161      4.11935]
      [ -3.45565     27.1554     -3.86714]
      [ 0.0299566   0.184309    -1.46709]]))
    (bitwise-not!)
    (u/mat-view))
```

The preceding filter turns the cat image into a mat ready to receive some brushes of watercolors (Figure 2-66).

Figure 2-66. *Artful cat*

Threshold

Threshold is another filtering technique that resets values in a mat to a default, when they are originally above or below a threshold.

Uh, what did you say?

To understand how that works, let's go back to a small mat at the pixel level again, with a simple 3×3 mat.

```
(u/matrix-to-mat [[0 50 100] [100 150 200] [200 210 250]])
; [0,    50,   100
;   100, 150,  200
;   200, 210,  250]
```

We can apply a threshold that sets the value of a pixel to

- 0, if the original pixel is below 150

- 250 otherwise

Here is how this works.

```
(->
  (u/matrix-to-mat [[0 50 100] [100 150 200] [200 210 250]])
  (threshold! 150 250 THRESH_BINARY)
  (.dump))
```

And the resulting matrix is

```
[0,    0,   0
  0,    0,   250
  250, 250, 250]
```

As you can see, only pixels with values greater than 150 are left to nonzero values.

You can create the complementary matrix by using THRESH_BINARY_INV, as seen in the following.

```
(->
  (u/matrix-to-mat [[0 50 100] [100 150 200] [200 210 250]])
  (threshold! 150 250 THRESH_BINARY_INV)
  (.dump))

; [250, 250, 250
    250, 250,   0
      0,   0,   0]
```

Now applying this technique to a picture makes things quite interesting by leaving only the interesting shapes of the content of the mat.

```
(-> "resources/emilie4.jpg"
  (imread)
  (cvt-color! COLOR_BGR2GRAY)
  (threshold! 150 250 THRESH_BINARY_INV)
  (u/mat-view))
```

Figure 2-67 shows the resulting mat after applying the threshold to my sister's white cat.

Figure 2-67. *Thresholded cat*

For reference, and for the next chapter's adventures, there is also another method named adaptive-threshold, which computes the target value depending on the values from the surrounding pixels.

```
(-> "resources/emilie4.jpg"
  (imread)
  (u/resize-by 0.07)
  (cvt-color! COLOR_BGR2GRAY)
  (adaptive-threshold! 255 ADAPTIVE_THRESH_MEAN_C THRESH_BINARY
9 20)
  (u/mat-view))
```

- 255 is the resulting value if the threshold is validated.

- You have just seen THRESH_BINARY or THRESH_BINARY_INV

- 9 is the size of the neighboring area to consider

- 20 is a value subtracted from the sum

Figure 2-68 shows the result of the adaptive threshold.

Figure 2-68. *Adaptive cat*

Adaptive threshold is usually used in recipe 2-8 with blurring techniques that we will study very shortly.

2-7 Applying Simple Masking Techniques

Problem

Masks can be used in a variety of situations where you want to apply mat functions only to a certain part of a mat.

You would like to know how to create masks and how to put them into action.

Solution

We will review again the use of **in-range** to create masks based on colors.

Then, we will use **copy-to** and **bitwise-** to apply functions on the main mat, but only on pixels selected by the mask.

How it works

Let's start by picking a romantic rose from the garden and loading with imread.

```
(def rose
  (-> "resources/red_rose.jpg"
      (imread IMREAD_REDUCED_COLOR_2)))
(u/mat-view rose)
```

Figure 2-69 shows the flower that will be the source of this exercise.

Figure 2-69. *Rose*

To search for colors, as we have seen, let's first convert the rose to a different color space.

You know how to achieve this by now. Since the color we will be looking for is red, let's convert from RGB to HSV.

```
(def hsv
  (-> rose clone (cvt-color! COLOR_RGB2HSV)))
(u/mat-view hsv)
```

Figure 2-70. *Rose in HSV color space*

Let's then filter on red, and since the rose is a bit dark too, let's make low values for saturation and luminosity on the lower bound red.

```
(def lower-red  (new-scalar 120 30 15))
(def upper-red (new-scalar 130 255 255))

(def mask (new-mat))
(in-range hsv lower-red upper-red mask)

(u/mat-view mask)
```

We used that method notably in recipe 2-4, but we forgot to have a look at the created mask. Basically, the mask is a mat of the same size as the input of in-range, with pixels set to 0 where the source pixel is not in range and to 1 where it is in range. Here indeed, in-range works a bit like a threshold.

The resulting mask is shown in Figure 2-71.

Figure 2-71. *Mask of the red rose*

The mask can now be used along with **bitwise-and!** and the original source rose so that we copy pixels only where the mask mat has values not equal to 0.

```
(def res (new-mat))
(bitwise-and! rose res mask)
(u/mat-view res)
```

And now you have a resulting mat (Figure 2-72) of only the red part of the picture.

Figure 2-72. *Only the rose*

As a small exercise, we'll change the luminosity of the mat by using convert-to and with it apply the following formula on each pixel:

original*alpha+ beta

And so, the following code snippet just does that by calling convert-to.

```
(def res2 (new-mat))
(convert-to res res2 -1 1 100)
(u/mat-view res2)
```

The resulting masked rose is a slightly brighter version of the original rose (Figure 2-73).

Figure 2-73. *Bright rose*

Let's copy that resulting bright rose back to the original picture, or a clone of it (Figure 2-74).

```
(def cl (clone rose))
(copy-to res2 cl mask)
(u/mat-view cl)
```

Figure 2-74. *Coming together*

The concepts are nicely coming together.

Finally, let's try something different, for example, copying a completely different mat in place of the rose, again using a mask.

We can reuse the mask that was created in the preceding, and in a similar fashion use copy-to to copy only specific points of a mat.

To perform the copy, we need the source and the target in copy-to to be of the exact same size, as well as the mask. You will get quite a bad error when this is not the case.

The resizing of mat is done as a first step.

```
(def cl2
  (imread "resources/emilie1.jpg"))
(resize! cl2 (new-size (cols mask) (rows mask)))
```

Then, on a clone of the original rose picture, we can perform the copy, specifying the mask as the last parameter of copy-to.

```
(def cl3
  (clone rose))
(copy-to cl2 cl3 mask)
(u/mat-view cl3)
```

The cat mat is thus copied onto the rose, but only where the mask allows the copy to happen (Figure 2-75).

Figure 2-75. *The cat and the rose*

2-8 Blurring Images

I'm giving in to my tendency to want to blur and blend the lines between art and life [...]

Lia Ices

Problem

As promised, this is a recipe to review blur techniques. *Blurring* is a simple and frequent technique used in a variety of situations.

You would like to see the different kinds of blur available, and how to use them with Origami.

Solution

There are four main methods to blur in OpenCV: **blur**, **gaussian-blur**, **median-blur**, and **bilateral-filter**.

Let's review each of them one by one.

How it works

As usual, let's load a base cat picture to use throughout this exercise.

```
(def neko
  (-> "resources/emilie5.jpg"
      (imread)
      (u/resize-by 0.07)))
(u/mat-view neko)
```

Figure 2-76 shows another picture of my sister's cat.

Figure 2-76. *Cat on bed*

Simple Blur and Median Blur

The flow to apply a simple **blur** is relatively simple. Like many other image-processing techniques, we use a kernel, a square matrix with the main pixel in the center, like 3×3 or 5×5. The kernel is the matrix in which each pixel is given a coefficient.

In its simplest form, we just need to give it a kernel size for the area to consider for the blur: the bigger the kernel area, the more blurred the resulting picture will be.

Basically, each pixel of the output is the mean of its kernel neighbors.

```
(-> neko
    (clone)
    (blur! (new-size 3 3))
    (u/mat-view))
```

The result can be seen in Figure 2-77.

Figure 2-77. *Blurred cat on bed*

And the bigger the kernel, the more blurred the picture will be.

Figure 2-78 shows the result of using different kernel sizes with the blur function.

```
(->> (range 3 10 2)
     (map #(-> neko  clone (u/resize-by 0.5) (blur! (new-size % %))))
     (hconcat!)
     (u/mat-view))
```

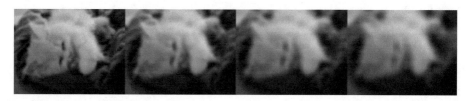

Figure 2-78. *Bigger kernels*

Gaussian Blur

This type of blur gives more weight to the center of the kernel. We will see that in the next chapter, but this type of blur is actually good at removing extra noise from pictures.

```
(-> neko clone (gaussian-blur! (new-size 5 5) 17) (u/mat-view))
```

The result of the gaussian blur is shown in Figure 2-79.

Figure 2-79. *Gaussian blurred cat*

Bilateral Filter

Those filters are used when you want to smooth the picture, but at the same time would also like to keep the edges.

What are edges? Edges are **contours** that define the shapes available in a picture.

The first example shows a simple usage of this bilateral filter.

```
(-> neko
    clone
    (bilateral-filter! 9 9 7)
    (u/mat-view))
```

Figure 2-80. *Gaussian blur*

This second example shows an example where we want to keep the edges. Edges can be easily found with the famous opencv function canny. We will spend some more time with canny in the next chapter.

For now, let's focus on the output and lines of Figure 2-81.

```
(-> neko
    clone
    (cvt-color! COLOR_BGR2GRAY)
    (bilateral-filter! 9 9 7)
```

```
(canny! 50.0 250.0 3 true)
(bitwise-not!)
(u/mat-view))
```

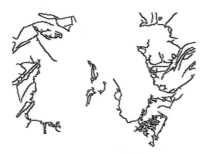

Figure 2-81. *Gaussian blur and canny*

The third example quickly shows why you would want to use a bilateral filter instead of a simple blur. We keep the same small processing pipeline but this time use a simple blur instead of a bilateral filter.

```
(-> neko
  clone
  (cvt-color! COLOR_BGR2GRAY)
  (blur! (new-size 3 3))
  (canny! 50.0 250.0 3 true)
  (bitwise-not!)
  (u/mat-view))
```

The output clearly highlights the problem: defining lines have disappeared, and Figure 2-82 shows a disappearing cat …

Figure 2-82. *Lines and cats have disappeared!*

Median Blur

Median blur is a friend of simple blur.

```
(-> neko
    clone
    (median-blur! 27)
    (u/mat-view))
```

It is worth noting that at high kernel length, or a kernel length of greater than 21, we get something more artistic.

It is less useful for shape detection, as seen in Figures 2-83 and 2-84, but still combines with other mats for creative impact, as we will see in chapter 3.

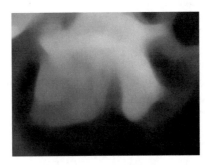

Figure 2-83. *Artistic cat (kernel length 31)*

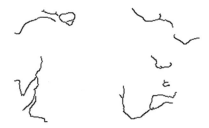

Figure 2-84. *Median blur with kernel 7 makes lines disappear*

Voila! Chapter 2 has been an introduction to Origami and its ease of use: the setup, the conciseness, the processing pipelines, and the various transformations.

This is only the beginning. Chapter 3 will be taking this setup to the next level by combining principles and functions of OpenCV to find shapes, count things, and move specific parts of mats to other locations.

The future belongs to those who prepare for it today.

Malcolm X

CHAPTER 3

Imaging Techniques

The most perfect technique is that which is not noticed at all.

Pablo Casals

The previous chapter was an introduction to Origami and how to perform mostly single-step processing operations on simple mats and images.

While that was already a very good show to highlight the library's ease of use, the third chapter wants to take you one step further by combining simple processing steps together to reach a bigger goal. From performing content analysis, contour detection, shape finding, and shape movements, all the way to computer-based sketching and landscape art, you name it, many an adventure awaits here.

We will start again on familiar ground by manipulating OpenCV mats at the byte level, to grasp in even more detail the ins and outs of image manipulation.

The learning will be split into two big sections. First will be a slightly art-focused section, where we play with lines, gradations, and OpenCV functions to create new images from existing ones. You will be using already known origami/opencv functions, but a few other ones will also be introduced as needed to go with the creative flow.

© Nicolas Modrzyk 2018
N. Modrzyk, *Java Image Processing Recipes*, https://doi.org/10.1007/978-1-4842-3465-5_3

It was one of the original plans of Origami to be used to create drawings. It just happened that to understand how simple concepts were brought together, I had to play with image compositions and wireframes that actually came out better than I thought they would. Even more so, it was easy to just add your own touch and reuse the creations later on. So that first part is meant to share this experience.

Then, in a second part, we will move onto techniques more focused on image processing. Processing steps will be easier to grasp at that stage, after reviewing steps with immediate feedback from the art section.

Processing steps in OpenCV are easy most of the time, but the original samples in C++ make it quite hard to read through the lines of pointers. I personally find, even with the Clojure learning curve included, that Origami is an easier way to get started with OpenCV: you can focus on the direct impact of your lines of code, and try writing each step in different ways without restarting everything by getting instant feedback each time, until eventually it comes into place nicely. Hopefully, the second part of the chapter will make you comfortable enough that you will want to go and challenge the examples even more.

Note that it is probably a good idea to read this chapter linearly so that you do not miss new functions or new tricks along the way. However, nothing prevents you from just jumping in where you feel like it, of course. It is a recipe book after all!

3-1 Playing with Colors
Problem

In the previous chapter, you already saw various techniques to change colors in a mat.

You would like to get control over how to specify and impact colors, for example, increasing or decreasing their intensity, by applying specific factors or functions on the mats.

Solution

Here, you will learn about the following: how to combine operations like converting an image color channel using the already known cvt-color; how to use other OpenCV functions like **threshold** to limit channel values; how to create masks and use them with the function **set-to**; and how to use functions to combine separate versions of a mat.

You will review also in more detail how to use the **transform!** function to create basic art effects.

How it works

To play with mats, we will be using another set of cats and flowers, but you can of course try applying the functions on your own photos any time.

The namespace header of the chapter, with all the namespace dependencies, will use the same namespaces required in the last chapter, namely, opencv3.core and opencv3.utils as well as opencv3.colors.rgb from origami's opencv3 original namespaces.

The required section looks like the following code snippet.

```
(ns opencv3.chapter03
(:require
 [opencv3.core :refer :all]
 [opencv3.colors.rgb :as rgb]
 [opencv3.utils :as u]))
```

It is usually a good idea to create a new notebook for each experiment, and to save them separately.

Applying Threshold on a Colored Mat

Back to the basics. Do you remember how to threshold on a mat, and keep only the values in the matrix above 150?

Yes, you're correct: use the threshold function.

```
(-> (u/matrix-to-mat [[100 255 200]
                      [100 255 200]
                      [100 255 200]])
    (threshold! 150 255 THRESH_BINARY)
    (dump))
```

The input matrix contains various values, some below and some above the threshold value of 150. When applying threshold, the values below are set to 0 and the ones above are set to threshold's second parameter value, 255.

This results in the following matrix (Figure 3-1):

```
[0 255 255]
[0 255 255]
[0 255 255]
```

Figure 3-1. *Black and white mat*

That was for a one-channel mat, but what happens if we do the same on a three-channel mat?

```
(-> (u/matrix-to-mat [[0 0 170]
                      [0 0 170]
                      [100 100 0]])
    (cvt-color! COLOR_GRAY2BGR)
    (threshold! 150 255 THRESH_BINARY)
    (dump))
```

Converting the colors to BGR duplicates each of the values of the one-channel mat to the same three values on the same pixel.

Applying the OpenCV threshold function right afterward applies the threshold to all the values over each channel. And so the resulting mat loses the 100 values of the original mat and keeps only the 255 values.

```
[0 0 0 0 0 0 255 255 255]
[0 0 0 0 0 0 255 255 255]
[0 0 0 0 0 0 0 0 0]
```

A 3×3 matrix is a bit too small to show onscreen, so let's use resize on the input matrix first.

```
(-> (u/matrix-to-mat [[0 0 170]
                      [0 0 170]
                      [100 100 0]])
    (cvt-color! COLOR_GRAY2BGR)
    (resize! (new-size 50 50) 1 1 INTER_AREA)
    (u/mat-view))
```

Applying a similar threshold on the preceding mat keeps the light gray, which has a value above the threshold, but removes the darker gray by turning it to black.

```
(-> (u/matrix-to-mat [[0 0 170]
                      [0 0 170]
                      [100 100 0]])
       (cvt-color! COLOR_GRAY2BGR)
    (threshold! 150 255 THRESH_BINARY)
    (resize! (new-size 50 50) 0 0 INTER_AREA)
    (u/mat-view))
```

This gives us Figure 3-2.

Figure 3-2. *Thresholded!*

Notice the use of a specific interpolation parameter with resize, **INTER_AREA,** which nicely cuts the shape sharp, instead of interpolating and forcing a blur.

Just for some extra info, the default resize method gives something like Figure 3-3, which can be used in other circumstances, but this is not what we want here.

Figure 3-3. *Resize with default interpolation*

Anyway, back to the exercise, and you probably have it at this point: applying a standard threshold pushes forward vivid colors.

Let's see how that works on a mat loaded from an image, and let's load our first image of the chapter (Figure 3-4).

```
(def rose
  (imread "resources/chapter03/rose.jpg" IMREAD_REDUCED_COLOR_4))
```

Figure 3-4. *Some say love it is a river*

We start by applying the same threshold that was applied on the mat loaded from a matrix, but this time on the rose image.

```
(->
  original
  (clone)
  (threshold! 100 255 THRESH_BINARY)
  (u/mat-view))
```

You get a striking result! (Figure 3-5)

Figure 3-5. *Vivid colors*

In a nicely shot photograph, this actually gives you an artistic feeling that you can build upon for cards and Christmas presents!

Let's now apply a similar technique on a completely different image. We'll turn the picture to black and white first and see what the result is.

This time, the picture is of playful kittens, as shown in Figure 3-6.

```
(-> "resources/chapter03/ai6.jpg"
    (imread IMREAD_REDUCED_COLOR_2)
    (u/mat-view))
```

Figure 3-6. *Playful cats*

If you apply a similar threshold but on the grayscale version, something rather interesting happens.

```
(-> "resources/chapter03/ai6.jpg"
    (imread  IMREAD_REDUCED_GRAYSCALE_2)
    (threshold! 100 255 THRESH_BINARY)
    (u/mat-view))
```

The two cats are actually standing out and being highlighted (Figure 3-7).

Figure 3-7. *Playful, highlighted cats*

Cool; this means that the shape we wanted to stand out has been highlighted.

Something similar to this can be used to find out shapes and moving objects; more in recipe 3-6 and 3-7.

For now, and to keep things artistic, let's work on a small function that will turn all the colors under a given threshold to one color, and all the values above the threshold to another one.

We can achieve this by

- First, turning to a different color space, namely HSV

- creating a mask from the threshold applied with THRESH_BINARY setting

- creating a second mask from the threshold applied with THRESH_BINARY_INV setting, thus creating a mask with opposite values from the first one

- converting the two masks to gray, so they are only made of one channel

- setting the color of the work mat using set-to, following the first mask

- setting the color of the work mat using again set-to, but following the second mask

- That's it!

In coding happiness, we will create a **low-high!** function that does the algorithm described in the preceding.

The **low-high!** function is composed of cvt-color!, threshold, and set-to, all functions you already have seen.

```
(defn low-high!
  ([image t1 color1 color2 ]
  (let [_copy (-> image clone (cvt-color! COLOR_BGR2HSV))
        _work (clone image)
        _thresh-1 (new-mat)
        _thresh-2 (new-mat)]

    (threshold _copy _thresh-1 t1 255 THRESH_BINARY)
    (cvt-color! _thresh-1 COLOR_BGR2GRAY)
    (set-to _work color1 _thresh-1)

    (threshold _copy _thresh-2 t1 255 THRESH_BINARY_INV)
    (cvt-color! _thresh-2 COLOR_BGR2GRAY)
    (set-to _work color2 _thresh-2)
    _work)))
```

We will call it on the rose picture, with a threshold of 150 and a white smoke to light blue split.

```
(->
 (imread "resources/chapter02/rose.jpg" IMREAD_REDUCED_COLOR_4)
 (low-high! 150 rgb/white-smoke- rgb/lightblue-1)
 (u/mat-view))
```

Executing the preceding snippet gives us Figure 3-8.

Figure 3-8. *White on light blue rose*

Great. But, you ask, do we really need to create two masks for this? Indeed, you do not. You can do a bitwise operation perfectly on the first mask. To do this, simply comment out the second mask creation and use **bitwise-not!** before calling set-to the second time.

```
;(threshold _copy _thresh-2 t1 255 THRESH_BINARY_INV)
;(cvt-color! _thresh-2 COLOR_BGR2GRAY)
(set-to _work color2 (bitwise-not! _thresh-1))
```

From there, you could also apply thresholds on different color maps, or create ranges to use as threshold values.

Another idea here is, obviously, to just hot-space-queen-ize any picture.

In case you are wondering, the following snippet does that for you.

```
(def freddie-red (new-scalar 26 48 231))
(def freddie-blue (new-scalar 132 46 71))
(def bryan-yellow (new-scalar 56 235 255))
(def bryan-grey (new-scalar 186 185 181))
(def john-blue (new-scalar 235 169 0))
(def john-red (new-scalar 32 87 233))
(def roger-green (new-scalar 72 157 53))
(def roger-pink (new-scalar 151 95 226))
```

```
(defn queen-ize [mat thresh]
    (vconcat! [
    (hconcat!
    [(-> mat clone (low-high! thresh freddie-red freddie-blue))
     (-> mat clone (low-high! thresh john-blue john-red))])
    (hconcat!
    [(-> mat clone (low-high! thresh roger-pink roger-green ))
     (-> mat clone (low-high! thresh bryan-yellow bryan-
    grey))] )]))
```

This really just is calling low-high! four times, each time with colors from the Queen album *Hot Space*, from 1982.

And the old-fashioned result is shown in Figure 3-9.

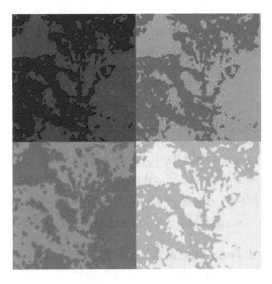

Figure 3-9. *Cats and Queen*

You really know how to set the mood

And you really get inside the groove

Cool cat

Queen – "Cool Cat"

Channels by Hand

Whenever you are about to play with channels of a mat, remember the opencv **split** function. The function separates the channels in a list of independent mats, so you can entirely focus on only one of them.

You can then apply transformations to that specific mat, without touching the others, and when finished, you can return to a multichannel mat using the **merge** function, which does the reverse and takes a list of mats, one per channel, and creates a target mat combining all the channels into one mat.

To see that in action, suppose you have a simple orange mat (Figure 3-10).

```
(def orange-mat
  (new-mat 3 3 CV_8UC3 rgb/orange-2))
```

Figure 3-10. *Orange mat*

If you want to turn the orange mat into a red one, you would simply set all the values of the green channel to 0.

So, you start by splitting the RGB channels into three mats; then, set all the values of the second mat to 0 and merge all three mats into one.

First, let's split the mat into channels, and see the content of each of them.

In happy coding, this gives

```
(def channels (new-arraylist))
(split orange-mat channels)
```

The three channels are now separated into three elements in the list. You can look at the content of each channel simply by using dump.

For example, dump of the blue channel:

```
(dump (nth channels 0))
```

```
; no blue
;[0 0 0]
;[0 0 0]
;[0 0 0]
```

or dump of the green channel:

```
(dump (nth channels 1))
```

```
; quite a bit of green
;[154 154 154]
;[154 154 154]
;[154 154 154]
```

Finally, dump of the red channel:

```
(dump (nth channels 2))
```

```
; almost max of red
;[238 238 238]
;[238 238 238]
;[238 238 238]
```

From there, let's turn all those 154 values in the green channel to 0.

```
(set-to (nth channels 1) (new-scalar 0.0))
```

And then, let's merge all the different mats back to a single mat and get Figure 3-11.

```
(merge channels red-mat)
```

Figure 3-11. *Red mat*

The green intensity on all pixels in the mat was uniformly set to 0, and so with all the blue channel values already set to 0, the resulting mat is a completely red one.

We can combine all the different steps of this small exercise and create the function **update-channel!,** which takes a mat, a function, and the channel to apply the function to and then returns the resulting mat.

Let's try a first version using **u/mat-to-bytes** and **u/bytes-to-mat!** to convert back and forth between mat and byte arrays.

This gets complicated, but is actually the easiest version I could come up with to explain the flow of the transformation.

The code flow will be as follows:

- split the channels into a list

- retrieve the target channel's mat

- convert the mat to bytes

- apply the function to every byte of the channel mat

- turn the byte array back to a mat

- set that mat to the corresponding channels in the list

- merge the channels into the resulting mat

This should now, at least, read almost sequentially as in the following:

```
(defn update-channel! [mat fnc chan]
  (let [ channels (new-arraylist)]
    (split mat channels)
```

```
(let [
  old-ch (nth channels chan)
  new-ch
(u/bytes-to-mat!
  (new-mat (.height mat) (.width mat) (.type old-ch) )
    (byte-array (map fnc (u/mat-to-bytes old-ch) )))]
  (.set channels chan new-ch)
  (merge channels mat)
  mat)))
```

Now let's get back to my sister's cat, who's been sleeping on the couch for some time. Time to tease him a bit and wake him up.

```
(def my-sister-cat
(-> "resources/chapter03/emilie1.jpg"
(imread IMREAD_REDUCED_COLOR_8)))
```

With the help of the update-channel! function, let's turn all the blue and green channel values to their maximum possible values of 255. We could have written a function that applies multiple functions at the same time, but for now let's just call the same function one by one in a row.

```
(->
  my-sister-cat
  clone
  (update-channel! (fn [x] 255) 1)
  (update-channel! (fn [x] 255) 0)
u/mat-view)
```

This is not very useful as far as imaging goes, nor very useful for my sister's cat either, but by maxing out all the values of the blue and green channels, we get a picture that is all cyan (Figure 3-12).

Figure 3-12. *Cyan cat*

This newly created function can also be combined with converting colorspace.

Thus, switching to HSV color space before calling **update-channel!** gives you full control over the mat's color.

```
(->
  my-sister-cat
  clone
  (cvt-color! COLOR_RGB2HSV)
  (update-channel! (fn [x] 10) 0) ; blue filter
  (cvt-color! COLOR_HSV2RGB)
  (u/mat-view))
```

The preceding code applies a blue filter, leaving saturation and brightness untouched, thus still keeping the image dynamics.

Of course, you could try with a pink filter, setting the filter's value to 150, or red, by setting the filter's value to 120, or any other possible value. Try it out!

For now, enjoy the blue variation in Figure 3-13.

191

Figure 3-13. *Blue-filtered cat*

Personally, I also like the YUV switch combined with maximizing all the luminance values (Y).

```
(->
  my-sister-cat
  clone
  (cvt-color! COLOR_BGR2YUV)
  (update-channel! (fn [x] 255) 0)
  (cvt-color! COLOR_YUV2BGR)
  (u/mat-view))
```

This gives a kind of watercolor feel to the image (Figure 3-14).

Figure 3-14. *Artful cat*

Transform

If you remember transform, you could also apply different sorts of transformation using the opencv transform function.

To understand the background of transform a bit, let's get back once again to the usual byte-per-byte matrix manipulation, first on a one-channel 3×3 mat that we would like to make slightly darker.

```
(def s-mat (new-mat 3 3 CV_8UC1))
(.put s-mat 0 0 (byte-array [100 255 200
                             100 255 200
                             100 255 200]))
```

This can be viewed with the following code (Figure 3-15).

Figure 3-15. *Flag in black and white*

```
(u/mat-view (-> s-mat clone (resize! (new-size 30 30) 1 1
INTER_AREA)))
```

Then we define a 1×1 transformation matrix, with one value of 0.7.

```
(def t-mat
  (new-mat 1 1 CV_32F (new-scalar 0.7))
```

Next, we apply the transformation in place and also dump the result to see the values out from the transformation.

```
(-> s-mat
    (transform! t-mat)
    (dump))
```

Calling the transform function has the effect of turning all the values of the input matrix to their original value multiplied by 0.7.

The result is shown in the following matrix:

$$\begin{bmatrix} 70 & 178 & 140 \end{bmatrix}$$
$$\begin{bmatrix} 70 & 178 & 140 \end{bmatrix}$$
$$\begin{bmatrix} 70 & 178 & 140 \end{bmatrix}$$

It also means that the visuals of the mat have become darker (Figure 3-16):

Figure 3-16. *Darker flag*

```
(u/mat-view (-> s-mat (resize! (new-size 30 30) 1 1 INTER_AREA)))
```

This is a simple matrix computation, but it already shows two things:

- The bytes of the source mat are all multiplied by the value in the 1×1 mat;

- It's actually easy to apply custom transformation.

Those transformations work much the same for mats with multiple channels. So, let's grab an example and move to a colored colorspace (yeah, I know) using cvt-color!

```
(def s-mat (new-mat 3 3 CV_8UC1))
(.put s-mat 0 0 (byte-array [100 255 200
                             100 255 200
                             100 255 200]))
(cvt-color! s-mat COLOR_GRAY2BGR)
```

194

Because the mat is now made of three channels, we now need a 3×3 transformation matrix.

The following transformation mat will give more strength to the blue channel.

```
[ 2 0 0  ; B -> B G R
  0 1 0  ; G -> B G R
  0 0 1] ; R -> B G R
```

The transformation matrix is made of lines constructed as input-channel -> output channel, so three values per row, one for each output value of each channel, and three rows, one for each input.

- [2 0 0] boosts the values of the blue channel by 2, and does not affect green or red output values

- [0 1 0] keeps the green channel as is, and does not contribute to other channels in the output

- [0 0 1] keeps the red channel as is, and similarly does not contribute to other channels in the output

```
(def t-mat (new-mat 3 3 CV_32F))
(.put t-mat 0 0 (float-array [2 0 0
                              0 1 0
                              0 0 1]))
```

Applying the transformation to the newly colored mat gives you Figure 3-17, where blue is prominently standing out.

Figure 3-17. *Blue flag*

Since there is definitely no way we can leave my sister's cat in peace, let's apply a similar transformation to it.

The code is exactly the same as the preceding small mat example, but applied on an image.

```
(-> my-sister-cat
  clone
  (transform! (u/matrix-to-mat [ [2 0 0] [0 1 0] [0 0 1]])))
```

And Figure 3-18 shows a blue version of a usually white cat.

Figure 3-18. *Blue meeoooww*

If you wanted blue in the input to also influence red in the output, you could use a matrix slightly similar to the following:

```
[2 0 1.1
 0 1 0
 0 0 1  ]
```

You can understand why by now, right? [2 0 1.1] means that the blue in the input is gaining intensity, but that it also contributes to the intensity of red in the output.

You should probably try a few transformation matrices by yourself to get a feel for them.

So, now, how could you increase the luminosity of a mat using a similar technique?

Yes, that's right: by converting the matrix to HSV colorspace first, then multiplying the third channel and keeping the others as they are.

The following sample increases the luminosity by 1.5 in the same fashion.

```
(-> my-sister-cat
clone
(cvt-color! COLOR_BGR2HSV)
(transform! (u/matrix-to-mat [ [1 0 0] [0 1 0] [0 0 1.5]]))
(cvt-color! COLOR_HSV2BGR)
u/mat-view)
```

Figure 3-19 shows the image output of the preceding snippet.

Figure 3-19. *Luminous cat*

Artful Transformations

To conclude this recipe, let's play a bit with luminosity and contours to create something a bit artistic.

We want to create a watercolor version of the input picture, by maximizing the luminosity. We also want to create a "contour" version of the image, by using opencv's canny quick feature of contour detection. Then finally, we will combine the two mats for a pencil-over-watercolor effect.

First, let's work on the background. The background is created by performing two transformations in a row: one to max out the luminosity in the YUV color space, the other to get it more vivid by increasing blue and red colors.

```
(def
  usui-cat
  (-> my-sister-cat
  clone
  (cvt-color! COLOR_BGR2YUV)
  (transform! (u/matrix-to-mat [
                  [20 0 0]
                  [0 1 0]
                  [0 0 1]]))
  (cvt-color! COLOR_YUV2BGR)
  (transform! (u/matrix-to-mat [[3 0 0]
                                [0 1 0]
                                [0 0 2]]))))
```

If you get a result that is too transparent, you could also add another transformation at the end of the pipeline to increase contrast; this is easily done in another colorspace, HSV.

```
(cvt-color! COLOR_BGR2HSV)
(transform! (u/matrix-to-mat
                     [[1 0 0]
                      [0 3 0]
                      [0 0 1]]))
(cvt-color! COLOR_HSV2BGR)
```

This gives us a nice pink-y background (Figure 3-20).

Figure 3-20. *Pink cat for background*

Next is the foreground. The front cat is created using a call to opencv's canny function. This time, this is done in the one-channel gray color space.

```
(def
  line-cat
  (-> my-sister-cat
      clone
  (cvt-color! COLOR_BGR2GRAY)
  (canny! 100.0 150.0 3 true)
  (cvt-color! COLOR_GRAY2BGR)
  (bitwise-not!)))
```

The canny version of my sister's cat gives the following (Figure 3-21):

Figure 3-21. *Cartoon cat*

Then, the two mats are combined using a simple call to the function **bitwise-and**, which merges two mats together by doing simple "and" bit operations.

```
(def target (new-mat))
(bitwise-and usui-cat line-cat target)
```

This gives the nice artful cat in Figure 3-22.

Figure 3-22. *Pink and art and cat*

While the pink color may not be your favorite, you now have all the tools to modify to your liking the flows presented in this recipe to create many variations of artful cats, with different background colors and also different foregrounds.

But please. No dogs.

3-2 Creating Cartoons

Be yourself. No one can say you're doing it wrong.

Charles M. Schulz

Problem

You have seen a very simple way of doing cartoon artwork using **canny**, but you would like to master a few more variations of doing cartoony artwork.

Solution

Most of the cartoon-looking transformations can be creating using a variation of grayscale, blur, canny, and the channel filter functions that were seen in the previous recipe.

How it works

You have already seen the canny function, famous for easily highlighting shapes in a picture. It can actually also be used for cartooning a bit. Let's see that with my friend Johan.

Johan is a sharp Belgian guy who sometimes gets tricked into having a glass of good Pinot Noir (Figure 3-23).

Figure 3-23. *Johan*

In this recipe, Johan was loaded with the following snippet:

```
(def source
  (-> "resources/chapter03/johan.jpg"
  (imread IMREAD_REDUCED_GRAYSCALE_8)))
```

A naïve canny call would look like this, where 10.0 and 90.0 are the bottom and top thresholds for the canny function, 3 is the aperture, and true/false means basically superhighlight mode or standard (false).

```
(->
source
clone
(canny! 10.0 90.0 3 false))
```

Johan has now been turned into a canny version of himself (Figure 3-24).

Figure 3-24. *Naïve canny usage*

You already know that we can use the result of the canny function as a mask and for example do a copy of blue over white (Figure 3-25).

```
(def colored (u/mat-from source))
(set-to colored rgb/blue-2)

(def target (u/mat-from source))
(set-to target rgb/white)

(copy-to colored target c)
```

Figure 3-25. *Copy blue over white*

That is quite a few lines showing in the picture. By reducing the range between the two threshold values, we can make the picture significantly clearer and look less messy.

```
(canny! 70.0 90.0 3 false)
```

This indeed makes Johan a bit clearer (Figure 3-26).

Figure 3-26. *Clearer Johan*

The result is nice, but it still seems that there are quite a few extra lines that should not be drawn.

The technique usually used to remove those extra lines is to apply a **median-blur** or a **gaussian-blur** before calling the canny function.

Gaussian blur is usually more effective; do not hesitate to go big and increase the size of the blur to at least 13×13 or even 21×21, as shown in the following:

```
(->
source
clone
(cvt-color! COLOR_BGR2GRAY)
(gaussian-blur! (new-size 13 13) 1 1)
(canny! 70.0 90.0 3 false))
```

That code snippet gives a neatly clearer picture (Figure 3-27).

Figure 3-27. *Even better Johan*

Do you remember the bilateral filter function? If you use it *after* calling the canny function, it also gives some interesting cartoon shapes, by putting emphasis where there are more lines coming out of the canny effect.

```
(->
 source
 clone
 (cvt-color! COLOR_BGR2GRAY)
 (canny! 70.0 90.0 3 false)
 (bilateral-filter! 10 80 30)))
```

Figure 3-28 shows the bilateral-filter! applied through a similar processing pipeline.

Figure 3-28. *Applying a bilateral filter*

You would remember that the focus of the bilateral filter is on reinforcing the contours. And indeed, that is what is achieved here.

Note also that the bilateral filter parameters are very sensitive, increasing the second parameter to 120; this gives a Picasso-like rendering (Figure 3-29).

Figure 3-29. *Johasso*

So, play around with parameters and see what works for you. The whole Origami setup is there to give immediate feedback anyway.

Also, canny is not the only option. Let's see other techniques to achieve cartoon effects.

Bilateral Cartoon

The bilateral filter is actually doing a lot of the cartoon work, so let's see if we can skip the canny processing and stick with just using the bilateral filter step.

We will create a new function called cartoon-0. That new function will

- turn the input image to gray

- apply a very large bilateral filter

- apply successive smoothing functions

- then turn back to an RGB mat

A possible implementation is shown in the following:

```
(defn cartoon-0!
  [buffer]
  (-> buffer
    (cvt-color! COLOR_RGB2GRAY)
    (bilateral-filter! 10 250 30)
    (median-blur! 7)
    (adaptive-threshold! 255 ADAPTIVE_THRESH_MEAN_C THRESH_
    BINARY 9 3)
    (cvt-color! COLOR_GRAY2BGR)))
```

The output of cartoon-0! applied to Johan makes it to Figure 3-30.

```
(-> "resources/chapter03/johan.jpg"
(imread IMREAD_REDUCED_COLOR_8)
cartoon-0!
u/mat-view)
```

Figure 3-30. *No canny cartoon*

Here again, the parameters of the bilateral filter pretty much make all the work.

Changing **(bilateral-filter! 10 250 30)** to **(bilateral-filter! 9 9 7)** gives a completely different feeling.

```
(defn cartoon-1!
  [buffer]
  (-> buffer
    (cvt-color! COLOR_RGB2GRAY)
    (bilateral-filter! 9 9 7)
    (median-blur! 7)
    (adaptive-threshold! 255 ADAPTIVE_THRESH_MEAN_C THRESH_
    BINARY 9 3)
    (cvt-color! COLOR_GRAY2BGR)))
```

And Johan now looks even more artistic and thoughtful (Figure 3-31).

Figure 3-31. *Thoughtful Johan*

Grayed with Update Channel

The last technique of this recipe will take us back to use the **update-channel!** function written in the previous recipe.

This new method uses update-channel with a function that

- turns the gray channel's value to 0 if the original value is less than 70;

- turns it to 100 if the original value is greater than 80 but less than 180; and

- turns it to 255 otherwise.

This gives the following slightly long but simple pipeline:

```
(->
  "resources/chapter03/johan.jpg"
  (imread IMREAD_REDUCED_COLOR_8)
  (median-blur! 1)
  (cvt-color! COLOR_BGR2GRAY)
  (update-channel! (fn[x] (cond (< x 70) 0 (< x 180) 100 :else 255)) 0)
  (bitwise-not!)
  (cvt-color! COLOR_GRAY2BGR)
  (u/mat-view))
```

This is nothing you would not understand by now, but the pipeline is quite a pleasure to write and its result even more so, because it gives more depth to the output than the other techniques used up to now (Figure 3-32).

Figure 3-32. *In-depth Johan*

The output of the pipeline looks great, but the pixels have had quite a bit of processing, so it is hard to tell what's inside each of them at this stage, and postprocessing after that needs a bit of care.

Say you want to increase the luminosity or change the color of the preceding output; it is usually better to switch again to HSV color space and increase the luminosity before changing anything on the colors, as highlighted in the following:

```
(->
"resources/chapter03/shinji.jpg"
(imread IMREAD_REDUCED_COLOR_4)
(cartoon! 70 180 false)
(cvt-color! COLOR_BGR2HSV)
(update-channel! (fn [x] 250) 1)
(update-channel! (fn [x] 5) 0)
(cvt-color! COLOR_HSV2BGR)
(bitwise-not!)
(flip! 1)
(u/mat-view))
```

The final processing pipeline gives us a shining blue Johan (Figure 3-33). The overall color is blue due to channel 0's value set to 5 in HSV range, and the luminosity set to 250, almost the maximum value.

Figure 3-33. *Flipped and blue*

As a bonus, we also just flipped the image horizontally to end this recipe on a forward-looking picture!

3-3 Creating Pencil Sketches
Problem

You have seen how to do some cartooning for portraits, but would like to give it a more artistic sense by combining front sketching with deep background colors.

Solution

To create backgrounds with impact, you will see how to use pyr-down and pyr-up combined with smoothing methods you have already seen.

To merge the result, we will again be using **bitwise-and**.

How it works

My hometown is in the French Alps, near the Swiss border, and there is a very nice canal flowing between the houses right in the middle of the old town (Figure 3-34).

Figure 3-34. *Annecy, France, in the summertime*

The goal here is to create a painted-looking version of that picture. The plan is to proceed in three phases.

A goal without a plan is just a wish.

Antoine de Saint-Exupéry

Phase 1: we completely remove all the contours of the picture by smoothing out the edges and doing loops of decreasing the resolution of the picture. This will be the background picture.

Phase 2: We do the opposite, meaning we focus on the contours, by applying similar techniques to what was done in the cartoon recipe, where we turn the picture to gray, find all the edges, and give them as much depth as possible. This will be the front part.

Phase 3: Finally, we combine the results of phase 1 and phase 2 to get the painting effect that we are looking for.

Background

pyr-down! is probably new to you. This decreases the resolution of an image. Let's compare the mats before and after applying the change of resolution done by the following snippet.

```
(def factor 1)
(def work (clone img))

(dotimes [_ factor] (pyr-down! work))
```

Before:

```
#object[org.opencv.core.Mat 0x3f133cac "Mat [
431*431*CV_8UC3...]"]
```

After:

```
#object[org.opencv.core.Mat 0x3f133cac "Mat [
216*216*CV_8UC3...]"]
```

Basically, the resolution of the mat has been divided by 2, rounded to the pixel. (Yes, I have heard stories of 1/2 pixels before, but beware... those are not true!!)

Using a factor of 4, and thus applying the resolution downgrade four times, we get a mat that is now 27×27 and looks like the mat in Figure 3-35.

Figure 3-35. *Changed resolution*

To create the background effect, we actually need a mat of the same size as the original, so there is a need to resize the output to the size of the original.

The first idea is of course to simply try the usual resize! function:

```
(resize! work (.size img))
```

But that does result in something not very satisfying to the eyes. Figure 3-36 indeed shows some quite visible weird pixelization of the resized mat.

Figure 3-36. *Hmmm... resizing*

214

Let's try something else. There is a reverse function of pyr-down, named pyr-up, which doubles the resolution of a mat. To use it effectively, we can apply pyr-up in a loop, and loop the same number of times as done with pyr-down.

```
(dotimes [_ factor] (pyr-up! work))
```

The resulting mat is similar to Figure 3-36, but is much smoother, as shown in Figure 3-37.

Figure 3-37. *Smooth blurring*

The background is finalized by applying blur in the mat in between the pyr-down and pyr-up dance.

So:

```
(dotimes [_ factor] (pyr-down! work))
(bilateral-filter! work 11 11 7)
(dotimes [_ factor] (pyr-up! work))
```

The output is kept for later, and that's it for the background; let's move to the edge-finding part for the foreground.

Foreground and Result

The foreground is going to be mostly a copy-paste exercise of the previous recipe. You can of course create your own variation at this stage; we will use here a cartooning function made of a median-blur and an adaptive-threshold step.

```
(def edge
  (-> img
    clone
    (resize! (new-size (.cols output) (.rows output)))
    (cvt-color! COLOR_RGB2GRAY)
    (median-blur! 7)
    (adaptive-threshold! 255 ADAPTIVE_THRESH_MEAN_C THRESH_
    BINARY 9 7)
    (cvt-color! COLOR_GRAY2RGB)))
```

Using the old town image as input, this time you get a mat showing only the prominent edges, as shown in Figure 3-38.

Figure 3-38. *Edges everywhere*

To finish the exercise, we now combine the two mats using bitwise-and. Basically, since the edges are black, a bitwise-and operation keeps them black, and their values will be copied over as they are to the output mat.

This will have the consequence of copying the edges over unchanged onto the target result, and since the remaining part of the edges mat is made of white, bitwise-and will be the value of the other mat, and so the color of the background mat will take precedence.

```
(let [result (new-mat) ]
  (bitwise-and work edge result)
  (u/mat-view result))
```

This gives you the sketching effect of Figure 3-39.

Figure 3-39. *Sketching like the pros*

With the adaptive threshold step, you can tune the way the front sketching looks.

```
(adaptive-threshold! 255 ADAPTIVE_THRESH_MEAN_C THRESH_BINARY
  edges-thickness edges-number)
```

We used 9 as edges-thickness and 7 as edges-number in the first sketch; let's see what happens if we put those two parameters to 5.

This gives more space to the color of the background, by reducing the thickness of the edges (Figure 3-40).

Figure 3-40. *Thinner edges*

It's now up to you to play and improvise from there!

Summary

Finally, let's get you equipped with a ready-to-use sketch! function. This is an exact copy of the code that has been used up to now, with places for the most important parameters for this sketching technique:

- the factors, e.g., the number of loops in the dance, used to turn the resolution down and then turn it up again

- the parameters of the bilateral filter of the background

- the parameters of the adaptive threshold of the foreground

The sketch! function is made of smoothing! and edges!. First, let's use smoothing! to create the background.

```
(defn smoothing!
  [img factor filter-size filter-value]
  (let [ work (clone img) output (new-mat)]
  (dotimes [_ factor] (pyr-down! work))
  (bilateral-filter work output filter-size filter-size filter-value)
  (dotimes [_ factor] (pyr-up! output))
  (resize! output (new-size (.cols img) (.rows img)))))
```

Then edges! to create the foreground.

```
(defn edges!
  [img e1 e2 e3]
  (-> img
    clone
    (cvt-color! COLOR_RGB2GRAY)
    (median-blur! e1)
    (adaptive-threshold! 255 ADAPTIVE_THRESH_MEAN_C THRESH_
    BINARY e2 e3)
    (cvt-color! COLOR_GRAY2RGB)))
```

Finally, we can use sketch!, the combination of background and foreground.

```
(defn sketch!
  [ img s1 s2 s3 e1 e2 e3]
  (let [ output (smoothing! img s1 s2 s3) edge (edges! img e1 e2 e3)]
  (bitwise-and output edge output)
  output))
```

Calling sketch! is relatively easy. You can try the following snippet:

```
(sketch! 6 9 7  7 9 11)
```

And instantly turn the landscape picture of Figure 3-41 …

Figure 3-41. *Trees*

into the sketched version of Figure 3-42.

Figure 3-42. *Sketch landscape*

A few others have been put in the samples, but now is indeed the time to take your own pictures and give those functions and parameters a shot.

3-4 Creating a Canvas Effect

Problem

Creating landscape art seems to have no more secrets for you, but you would like to emboss a canvas onto it, to make it more like a painting.

Solution

This short recipe will reuse techniques you have seen, along with two new mat functions: **multiply** and **divide.**

With divide, it is possible to create burning and dodging effects of a mat, and we will use those to create the wanted effect.

With **multiply**, it is possible to combine mats back with a nice depth effect, and so by using a paper-looking background mat, it will be possible to have a special draw on canvas output.

How it works

We will take another picture from the French Alps—I mean why not!—and since we would like to make it look slightly vintage, we will use an image of an old castle.

```
(def img
  (-> "resources/chapter03/montrottier.jpg"
  (imread IMREAD_REDUCED_COLOR_4)))
```

Figure 3-43 shows the castle of Montrottier, which you should probably visit when you have the time, or vacation (I do not even know what the second word means anymore).

Figure 3-43. *Wish upon a star*

We first start by applying a **bitwise-not!**, then a **gaussian-blur** on a gray clone of the source picture; this is pretty easy to do with Origami pipelines.

We will need a grayed version for later as well, so let's keep the two mats gray and gaussed separate.

```
(def gray
  (-> img clone (cvt-color! COLOR_BGR2GRAY)))
(def gaussed
  (-> gray
      clone
      bitwise-not!
      (gaussian-blur! (new-size 21 21) 0.0 0.0)))
```

Figure 3-44 shows the gaussed mat, which looks like a spooky version of the input image.

Figure 3-44. *Spooky castle*

We will use this gaussed mat as a mask. The magic happens in the function **dodge!**, which uses the opencv function divide on the original picture, and an inverted version of the gaussed mat.

```
(defn dodge! [img_ mask]
  (let [ output (clone img_) ]
  (divide img_ (bitwise-not! (-> mask clone)) output 256.0)
  output))
```

Hmmm... okay. What does divide do? I mean, you know it divides things, but at the byte level, what is really happening?

Let's take two matrices, a and b, and call divide on them for an example.

```
(def a (u/matrix-to-mat [[1 1 1]]))
(def b (u/matrix-to-mat [[0 1 2]]))
(def c (new-mat))
(divide a b c 10.0)
(dump c)
```

The output of the divide call is

```
[0 10 5]
```

which is

`[ (a0 / b0) * 10.0, (a1 / b1) * 10.0, (a2 / b2) * 10.0]`

which gives

`[ 1 / 0 * 10.0, 1 / 1 * 10.0, 1 / 2 * 10.0]`

then, given that OpenCV considers that dividing by 0 equals 0:

`[0, 10, 5]`

Now, let's call dodge! on the gray mat and the gaussed mat:

`(u/mat-view (dodge! gray gaussed))`

And see the sharp result of Figure 3-45.

Figure 3-45. *Sharp pencil*

Apply the Canvas

Now that the main picture has been turned to a crayon-styled art form, it would be nice to lay this out on a canvas-looking mat. As presented, this is done using the **multiply** function from OpenCV.

We want the canvas to look like a very old parchment, and we will use the one from Figure 3-46.

Figure 3-46. *Old parchment*

Now we will create the **apply-canvas!** function, which takes the front-end sketch, and the canvas, and applies the multiply function between them. (/ 1 256.0) is the value used for the multiplication; since these are gray bytes here, the bigger the value the whiter, and so here (/ 1 256.0) makes the dark lines stand out quite nicely on the final result.

```
(defn apply-canvas! [ sketch canvas]
 (let [ out (new-mat)]
  (resize! canvas (new-size (.cols sketch) (.rows sketch)))
  (multiply
   (-> sketch clone (cvt-color! COLOR_GRAY2RGB)) canvas out
   (/ 1 256.0))
   out))
```

Whoo-hoo. Almost there; now let's call this newly created function

```
(u/mat-view (apply-canvas! sketch canvas))
```

And enjoy the drawing on the canvas (Figure 3-47).

Figure 3-47.   Castle on old Parchment

Now is obviously the time for you to go and find/scan your own old papers, to try a few things using this technique; or why not reuse the cartoon functions from previous recipes to lay on top of the different papers?

3-5 Highlighting Lines and Circles

Problem

This recipe is about teaching how to find and highlight lines, circles, and segments in a loaded mat.

Solution

A bit of preprocessing is usually needed to prepare the image to be analyzed with some canny and smoothing operations.

Once this first preparation step is done, finding circles is done with the opencv function hough-circles.

The version to find lines is called hough-lines, with its sibling hough-lines-p, which uses probability to find better lines.

Finally, we will see how to use a line-segment-detector to draw the found segments.

How it works

Find Lines of a Tennis Court with Hough-Lines

The first part of this tutorial shows how to find lines within an image. We will take the example of a tennis court.

```
(def tennis (-> "resources/chapter03/tennis_ground.jpg" imread ))
```

You have probably seen a tennis court before, and this one is not so different from the others (Figure 3-48). If you have never seen a tennis court before, this is a great introduction all the same, but you should probably stop reading and go play a game already.

Figure 3-48. *Tennis court*

Preparing the target for the hough-lines function is done by converting the original tennis court picture to gray, then applying a simple canny transformation.

```
(def can
    (-> tennis
        clone
        (cvt-color! COLOR_BGR2GRAY)
        (canny! 50.0 180.0 3 false)))
```

With the expected result of the lines standing out on a black background, as shown in Figure 3-49.

Figure 3-49. *Canny tennis court*

Lines are collected in a mat in the underlying Java version of opencv, and so, no way to avoid this, we will also prepare a mat to receive the resulting lines.

The hough-lines function itself is called with a bunch of parameters. The full underlying polar system explanation for the hough transformation can be found on the OpenCV web site:

```
https://docs.opencv.org/3.3.1/d9/db0/tutorial_hough_lines.html
```

You don't really need to read everything just now, but it's good to realize what can be done and what cannot.

For now, we will just apply the same parameters suggested in the linked tutorial.

```
(def lines (new-mat))
(hough-lines can lines 1 (/ Math/PI 180) 100)
```

The resulting mat of lines is made of a list of rows with two values, rho and theta, on each row.

Creating the two points required to draw a line from rho and theta is a bit complicated but is described in the opencv tutorial.

For now, the following function does the work for you.

```
(def result (clone parking))
(dotimes [ i (.rows lines)]
   (let [ val_ (.get lines i 0)
          rho (nth val_ 0)
          theta (nth val_ 1)
          a (Math/cos theta)
          b (Math/sin theta)
          x0 (* a rho)
          y0 (* b rho)
          pt1 (new-point
              (Math/round (+ x0 (* 1000 (* -1 b))))
              (Math/round (+ y0 (* 1000 a))))
          pt2 (new-point
              (Math/round (- x0 (* 1000 (* -1 b))))
              (Math/round (- y0 (* 1000 a))))
      ]
   (line result pt1 pt2 color/black 1)))
```

Drawing the found lines on top of the tennis court mat creates the image in Figure 3-50.

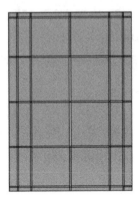

Figure 3-50. *Hough-lines result*

Note that when calling hough-lines, changing the parameter with value 1 to a value of 2 gives you way more lines, but you may need to filter the lines yourself afterward.

Also by experience, changing the Math/PI rounding from 180 to 90 gives fewer lines but better results.

Hough-Lines-P

Another variant of the hough-lines function, named hough-lines-p, is an enhanced version with probabilistic mathematics added, and it usually gives a better set of lines by performing guesses.

To try hough-lines with P, we will this time take the example of... a soccer field.

```
(def soccer-field
  (-> "resources/chapter03/soccer-field.jpg"
      (imread IMREAD_REDUCED_COLOR_4)))
(u/mat-view soccer-field)
```

As per the original hough-lines example, we turn the soccer field to gray and apply a slight gaussian blur to remove possible imperfections in the source image.

```
(def gray
  (-> soccer-field
      clone
      (cvt-color! COLOR_BGR2GRAY)
      (gaussian-blur! (new-size 1 1) 0 ) ))
```

The resulting grayed version of the soccer field is shown in Figure 3-51.

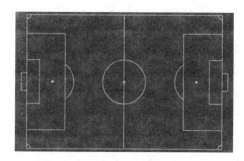

Figure 3-51. *Gray soccer field*

Let's now make a canny version of the court to create the edges.

```
(def edges (-> gray clone (canny! 100 220)))
```

Now, we call **hough-lines-p.** The parameters used are explained in line in the following code snippet. Lines are expected to be collected from the newly created edges mat.

```
; distance resolution in pixels of the Hough grid
(def rho 1)
; angular resolution in radians of the Hough grid
(def theta  (/ Math/PI 180))
; minimum number of votes (intersections in Hough grid cell)
(def min-intersections 30)
; minimum number of pixels making up a line
(def min-line-length  10)
```

```
; maximum gap in pixels between connectable line segments
(def max-line-gap  50)
```

The parameters are ready; let's call hough-lines-p, with the result being stored in the **lines** mat.

```
(def lines (new-mat))
(hough-lines-p
  edges
  lines
  rho
  theta
  min-intersections
  min-line-length
  max-line-gap)
```

This time, the lines are slightly easier to draw than with the regular hough-lines function. Each line of the result mat is made of four values, for the two points needed to draw the line.

```
(def result (clone soccer-field))
(dotimes [ i (.rows lines)]
(let [ val (.get lines i 0)]
  (line result
    (new-point (nth val 0) (nth val 1))
    (new-point (nth val 2) (nth val 3))
    color/black 1)))
```

The result of drawing the results of hough-lines-p is displayed in Figure 3-52.

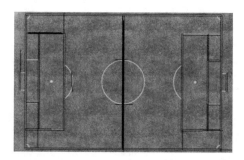

Figure 3-52. *Lines on a soccer field*

Finding Pockets on a Pool Table

No more running around on a court; let's move to... the billiard table!

In a similar way, opencv has a function named hough-circles to look for circle-looking shapes. What's more, the function is pretty easy to put in action.

This time, let's try to find the ball pockets of a billiard table. The exercise is slightly difficult because it is easy to wrongly count the regular balls as pockets.

> *You can't knock on opportunity's door and not be ready.*
>
> Bruno Mars

Let's get the pool table ready first.

```
(def pool
  (->
    "resources/chapter03/pooltable.jpg"
    (imread IMREAD_REDUCED_COLOR_2)))
```

With hough-circles, it seems you can actually get better results by bypassing the canny step in the preprocessing.

The following snippet now shows where to put values for the min and max radius of the circles to look for in the source mat.

```
(def gray (-> pool clone (cvt-color! COLOR_BGR2GRAY)))
(def minRadius 13)
(def maxRadius 18)
(def circles (new-mat))
(hough-circles gray circles CV_HOUGH_GRADIENT 1
  minRadius 120 10 minRadius maxRadius)
```

Here again, circles are collected in a mat, with each line containing the x and y position of the center of the circle and its radius.

Finally, we simply draw circles on the result mat with the opencv **circle** function.

```
(def output (clone pool))
(dotimes [i (.cols circles)]
  (let [ _circle (.get circles 0 i)
        x (nth _circle 0)
        y (nth _circle 1)
        r (nth _circle 2)
        p (new-point x y)]
(circle output p (int r) color/white 3)))
```

All the pockets are now highlighted in white in Figure 3-53.

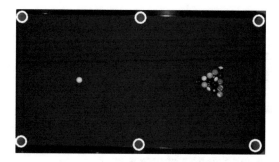

Figure 3-53. *Pockets of the pool table in white!*

Note that if you put the minRadius value too low, you quickly get false positives with the regular balls, as shown in Figure 3-54.

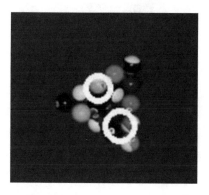

Figure 3-54. *False pockets*

So defining precisely what is searched for is the recipe for success in most of your OpenCV endeavors (and maybe other ones too...).

And so, to avoid false positives here, it is also probably a good idea to filter on colors before accepting and drawing the lines. Let's see how to do this next.

Finding Circles

In this short example, we will be looking for red circles in a mat where circles of multiple colors can be found.

```
(def bgr-image
  (-> "resources/detect/circles.jpg" imread (u/resize-by 0.5) ))
```

The bgr-image is shown in Figure 3-55.

Figure 3-55. *Colorful circles*

You may not see it if you are reading straight from the black-and-white version of the book, but we will be focusing on the large bottom left circle, which is of a vivid red.

If you remember lessons from the previous recipes, you already know we need to change the color space to HSV and then filter on a hue range between 0 and 10.

The following snippet shows how to do this along with some extra blurring to ease processing later on.

```
(def ogr-image
  (-> bgr-image
```

```
(clone)
(median-blur! 3)
(cvt-color! COLOR_BGR2HSV)
(in-range! (new-scalar 0 100 100) (new-scalar 10 255 255))
(gaussian-blur! (new-size 9 9) 2 2)))
```

All the circles we are not looking for have disappeared from the mat resulting from the small pipeline, and the only circle we are looking for is now standing out nicely (Figure 3-56).

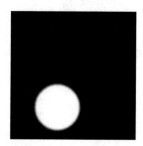

Figure 3-56. *Red circle showing in white*

Now we can apply the same hough-circles call as was seen just previously; again, the circle will be collected in the circle mat, which will be a 1×1 mat with three channels.

```
(def circles (new-mat))
(hough-circles ogr-image circles CV_HOUGH_GRADIENT 1 (/ (.rows
bgr-image) 8) 100 20 0 0)
(dotimes [i (.cols circles)]
  (let [ _circle (.get circles 0 i)
         x (nth _circle 0)
         y (nth _circle 1)
         r (nth _circle 2)
         p (new-point x y)]
    (circle bgr-image p (int r) rgb/greenyellow 5)))
```

The result of drawing the circle with a border is shown in Figure 3-57. The red circle has been highlighted with a green-yellow color and a thickness of 5.

Figure 3-57. *Highlighted red circle*

Using Draw Segment

Sometimes, the easiest may be to simply use a technique using the provided segment detector. It is less origami friendly, since the methods used are straight Java method calls (so prefixed with a dot "."), but the snippet is rather self-contained.

Let's try that on the previously seen soccer field. We'll load it straight to gray this time and see how the segment detector behaves.

```
(def soccer-field
    (-> "resources/chapter03/soccer-field.jpg"
    (imread IMREAD_REDUCED_GRAYSCALE_4)))

(def det (create-line-segment-detector))
(def lines (new-mat))
(def result (clone soccer-field))
```

We call **detect** on the line-segment-detector, using Clojure Java Interop for now.

```
(.detect det soccer-field lines)
```

At this stage, the lines mat metadata is 161*1*CV_32FC4, meaning 161 rows, each made of 1 column and 4 channels per dot, meaning 2 points per value.

The detector has a helpful drawSegments function, which we can call to get the resulting mat.

```
(.drawSegments det result lines)
```

The soccer field mat is now showing in Figure 3-58, this time with all the lines highlighted, including circles and semicircles.

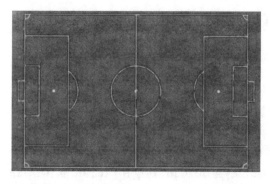

Figure 3-58. *Premiere mi-temps (first period)*

3-6 Finding and Drawing Contours and Bounding Boxes

Problem

Since identifying and counting shapes are at the forefront of OpenCV usage, you would probably like to know how to use contour-finding techniques in Origami.

Solution

Apart from the traditional cleanup and image preparation, this recipe will introduce the **find-contours** function to fill in a list of contours.

Once the contours are found, we need to apply a simple filter to remove extremely large contours like the whole pictures as well as contours that are really too small to be useful.

Once filtering is done, we can draw the contours using either handmade circles and rectangles or the provided function **draw-contours**.

How it works

Sony Headphones

They are not so new anymore, but I love my Sony headphones. I simply bring them everywhere, and you can feed your narcissism and get all the attention you need by simply wearing them. They also get you the best sound, whether on the train or on the plane...

Let's have a quick game of finding my headphones' contours.

```
(def headphones
  (-> "resources/chapter03/sonyheadphones.jpg"
      (imread IMREAD_REDUCED_COLOR_4)))
```

My headphones still have a cable, because I like the sound better still, whatever some big companies are saying.

Anyway, the headphones are shown in Figure 3-59.

Figure 3-59. *Sony headphones with a cable*

First, we need to prepare the headset to be easier to analyze. To do this, we create a mask of the interesting part, the headphones themselves.

```
(def mask
  (-> headphones
      (cvt-color! COLOR_BGR2GRAY)
      (clone)
      (threshold! 250 255 THRESH_BINARY_INV)
      (median-blur! 7)))
```

The inverted thresh binary output is shown in Figure 3-60.

Figure 3-60. *Masked headphones*

Then with the use of the mask, we create a masked-input mat that will be used to ease the finding contours step.

```
(def masked-input
  (clone headphones))
```

```
(set-to masked-input (new-scalar 0 0 0) mask)
(set-to masked-input (new-scalar 255 255 255) (bitwise-not!
mask))
```

Have you noticed? Yes, there was an easier way to create the input, by simply creating a noninverted mask in the first place, but this second method gives more control for preparing the input mat.

So here we basically proceed in two steps. First, set all the pixels of the original mat to black when the same pixel value of the mask is 1. Next, set all the other values to white, on the opposite version of the mask.

The prepared result mat is in Figure 3-61.

Figure 3-61. *Preparation of the input mat*

Now that the mat that will be used to find contours is ready, you can almost directly call find-contours on it.

find-contours takes a few obvious parameters, and two ones, the last two, that are a bit more obscure.

RETR_LIST is the simplest one, and returns all the contours as a list, while **RETR_TREE** is the most often used, and means that the contours are hierarchically ordered.

CHAIN_APPROX_NONE means all the points of the found contours are stored. Usually though, when drawing those contours, you do not need all of the points defining them. In case you do not need all of the points, you can use **CHAIN_APPROX_SIMPLE**, which reduces the number of points defining the contours.

It eventually depends how you handle the contours afterward. But for now, let's keep all the points!

```
(def contours
  (new-arraylist))

(find-contours
  masked-input
  contours
  (new-mat) ; mask
  RETR_TREE
  CHAIN_APPROX_NONE)
```

Alright, now let's draw rectangles to highlight each found contour. We loop on the contour list, and for each contour we use the **bounding-rect** function to get a rectangle that wraps the contour itself.

The rectangle retrieve from the bounding-rect call can be used almost as is, and we will draw our first contours with it.

```
(def exercise-1 (clone headphones))
(doseq [c contours]
  (let [ rect (bounding-rect c)]
  (rectangle
    exercise-1
    (new-point (.x rect) (.y rect))
```

```
(new-point (+ (.width rect) (.x rect)) (+ (.y rect)
(.height rect)))
(color/->scalar "#ccffcc")
2)))
```

Contours are now showing in Figure 3-62.

Figure 3-62. *Headphone coutours*

Right. Not bad. It is pretty obvious from the picture that the big rectangle spreading over the whole picture is not very useful. That's why we need a bit of filtering.

Let's filter the contours, by making sure they are

- not too small, meaning that the area they should cover is at least 10,000, which is a surface of 125×80,

- nor too big, meaning that the height shouldn't cover the whole picture.

That filtering is now done in the following snippet.

```
(def interesting-contours
  (filter
    #(and
        (> (contour-area %) 10000 )
        (< (.height (bounding-rect %)) (- (.height headphones) 10)))
    contours))
```

And so, drawing only the interesting-contours this time gives something quite accurate.

```
(def exercise-1 (clone headphones))
(doseq [c interesting-contours]
   ...)
```

Figure 3-63 this time shows only useful contours.

Figure 3-63. *Headphones' interesting contours*

Drawing circles instead of rectangles should not be too hard, so here we go with the same loop on interesting-contours, but this time, drawing a circle based on the bounding-rect.

```
(def exercise-2 (clone headphones))

(doseq [c interesting-contours]
 (let [ rect (bounding-rect c) center (u/center-of-rect rect) ]
   (circle exercise-2
           center
           (u/distance-of-two-points center (.tl rect))
           (color/->scalar "#ccffcc")
            2)))
```

The resulting mat, exercise-2, is shown in Figure 3-64.

Figure 3-64. *Circling on it*

Finally, while it's harder to use for detection processing, you can also use the opencv function **draw-contours** to nicely draw the free shape of the contour.

We will still be looping on the interesting-contours list. Note that the parameters may feel a bit strange, since draw-contours uses an index along with the list instead of the contour itself, so be careful when using draw-contours.

```
(def exercise-3 (clone headphones))

(dotimes [ci (.size interesting-contours)]
  (draw-contours
    exercise-3
    interesting-contours
    ci
    (color/->scalar "#cc66cc")
    3))
```

And finally, the resulting mat can be found in Figure 3-65.

Figure 3-65. *Headset and pink contours*

Things are not always so easy, so let's take another example up in the sky!

Up in the Sky

This second example takes hot-air balloons in the sky, and wants to draw contours on them.

The picture of hot-air balloons in Figure 3-66 seems very innocent and peaceful.

Figure 3-66. *Hot-air balloons*

Unfortunately, using the same technique as previously shown to prepare the picture does not reach a very sexy result.

```
(def wrong-mask
  (-> kikyu
      clone
      (cvt-color! COLOR_BGR2GRAY)
      (threshold! 250 255 THRESH_BINARY)
      (median-blur! 7)))
```

It's pretty pitch-black in Figure 3-67.

Figure 3-67. *Anybody up here?*

So, let's try another technique. What would you do to get a better mask?

Yes—why not? Let's filter all this blue and create a blurred mask from it. This should give you the following snippet.

```
(def mask
  (-> kikyu
      (clone)
      (cvt-color! COLOR_RGB2HSV)
      (in-range! (new-scalar 10 30 30) (new-scalar 30 255 255))
      (median-blur! 7)))
```

Nice! Figure 3-68 shows that this actually worked out pretty neatly.

Figure 3-68. *Useful mask*

We will now use the complement version of the mask to find the contours.

```
(def work (-> mask bitwise-not!))
```

Using the finding-contours function has no more secrets to hide from you. Or maybe it does? What's the **new-point** doing in the parameter list? Don't worry; it is just an offset value, and here we specify no offset, so 0 0.

```
(def contours (new-arraylist))
(find-contours work contours (new-mat) RETR_LIST CHAIN_APPROX_
SIMPLE (new-point 0 0))
```

Contours are in! Let's filter on the size and draw circles around them. This is simply a rehash of the previous example.

```
(def output_ (clone kikyu))

(doseq [c contours]
  (if (> (contour-area c) 50 )
    (let [ rect (bounding-rect c)]
      (if (and  (> (.height rect) 40)  (> (.width rect) 60))
      (circle
        output_
```

```
(new-point (+ (/ (.width rect) 2) (.x rect))
           (+ (.y rect) (/ (.height rect) 2)))
100
rgb/tan
5)))))
```

Nice. You are getting pretty good at those things. Look at and enjoy the result of Figure 3-69.

Figure 3-69. *Circles over the hot-air balloons*

Next, let's filter ahead of the drawing, and let's use the bounding-rect again to draw rectangles.

```
(def my-contours
  (filter
  #(and
  (> (contour-area %) 50 )
  (> (.height (bounding-rect %)) 40)
  (> (.width (bounding-rect %)) 60))
contours))
```

And yes indeed, if you checked its content, my-contours has only three elements.

```
(doseq [c my-contours]
  (let [ rect (bounding-rect c)]
    (rectangle
      output
      (new-point (.x rect) (.y rect))
      (new-point (+ (.width rect) (.x rect)) (+ (.y rect)
      (.height rect)))
      rgb/tan
      5)))
```

Now drawing those rectangles results in Figure 3-70.

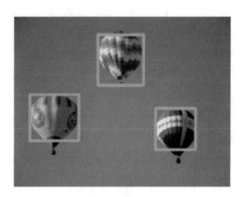

Figure 3-70. *Rectangles over hot-air balloons*

3-7 More on Contours: Playing with Shapes

Problem

Following on the previous recipe, you would like to see what's returned by the function find-contours. Drawing contours with all the dots is nice, but what if you want to highlight different shapes in different colors?

Also, what if the shapes are hand-drawn, or not showing properly in the source mat?

Solution

We still are going to use find-contours and draw-contours as we have done up to now, but we are going to do some preprocessing on each contour before drawing them to find out how many sides they have.

approx-poly-dp is the function that will be used to approximate shape, thus reducing the number of points and keeping only the most important dots of polygonal shapes. We will create a small function, **approx,** to turn shapes into polygons and count the number of sides they have.

We will also look at **fill-convex-poly** to see how we can draw the approximated contours of handwritten shapes.

Lastly, another opencv function named **polylines** will be used to draw only wireframes of the found contours.

How it works

Highlight Contours

We will use a picture with many shapes for the first part of this exercise, like the one in Figure 3-71.

Figure 3-71. *Shapes*

The goal here is to draw the contours of each shape with different colors depending on the number of sides of each shape.

The shapes mat is loaded simply with the following snippet:

```
(def shapes
  (-> "resources/morph/shapes3.jpg" (imread IMREAD_REDUCED_COLOR_2)))
```

As was done in the previous recipe, we first prepare a thresh mat from the input by converting a clone of the input to gray, then applying a simple threshold to highlight the shapes.

```
(def thresh (->
    shapes
    clone
    (cvt-color! COLOR_BGR2GRAY)
    (threshold! 210 240 1)))
(def contours (new-arraylist))
```

Looking closely, we can see that the shapes are nicely highlighted, and if you look at Figure 3-72, the thresh is indeed nicely showing the shapes.

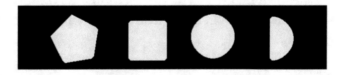

Figure 3-72. *Functional thresh*

Ok, the thresh is ready, so you can now call **find-contours** on it.

```
(find-contours thresh contours (new-mat) RETR_LIST CHAIN_
APPROX_SIMPLE)
```

To draw the contours, we first write a dump function that loops on the contours list and draws each one in magenta.

```
(defn draw-contours! [img contours]
  (dotimes [i (.size contours)]
    (let [c (.get contours i)]
     (draw-contours img contours i rgb/magenta-2 3)))
    img)

(-> shapes
      (draw-contours! contours)
      (u/mat-view))
```

The function works as expected, and the result is shown in Figure 3-73.

Figure 3-73. *Magenta contours*

But, as we have said, we would like to use a different color for each contour, so let's write a function that selects a color depending on the sides of the contour.

```
(defn which-color[c]
  (condp = (how-many-sides c)
    1 rgb/pink
```

```
2 rgb/magenta-
3 rgb/green
4 rgb/blue
5 rgb/yellow-1-
6 rgb/cyan-2
rgb/orange))
```

Unfortunately, even with **CHAIN_APPROX_SIMPLE** passed as parameter to find-contours, the number of points for each shape is way too high to make any sense.

```
8, 70, 132, 137...
```

So, let's work on reducing the number of points by converting the shapes to approximations.

Two functions are used from opencv, arc-length, and approx-poly-dp. The factor 0.02 is the default proposed by opencv; we will see its impact with different values slightly later in this recipe.

```
(defn approx [c]
  (let[m2f (new-matofpoint2f (.toArray c))
       len (arc-length m2f true)
       ret (new-matofpoint2f)
       app (approx-poly-dp m2f ret (* 0.02 len) true)]
    ret))
```

Using this new **approx** function, we can now count the number of sides by counting the number of points of the approximation.

The following is the how-many-sides function that simply does that.

```
(defn how-many-sides[c]
  (let[nb-sides (.size (.toList  c))]
    nb-sides))
```

Everything is in place; let's rewrite the dumb **draw-contours!** function into something slightly more evolved using which-color.

```
(defn draw-contours! [img contours]
  (dotimes [i (.size contours)]
    (let [c (.get contours i)]
      (draw-contours img contours i (which-color c) 3)))
    img)
```

And now calling the updated function properly highlights the polygons, counting the number of sides on an approximation of each of the found shapes (Figure 3-74).

Figure 3-74. *Different shapes, different colors*

Note how the circle still goes slightly overboard, with too many sides, but that was to be expected.

Hand-Drawn Shapes

But perhaps you were going to say that the shapes were nicely showing already, so you still have some doubts about whether the approximation is really useful or not. So, let's head to a beautiful piece of hand-drawn art that was prepared just for the purpose of this example.

```
(def shapes2
  (-> "resources/chapter03/hand_shapes.jpg"
      (imread IMREAD_REDUCED_COLOR_2)))
```

Figure 3-75 shows the newly loaded shapes.

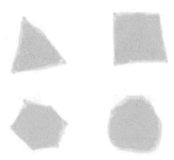

Figure 3-75. *Piece of art*

First, let's call find-contours and draw the shapes defined by them.

Reusing the same **draw-contours!** function and drawing over the art itself gives Figure 3-76.

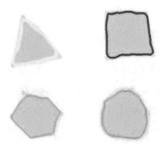

Figure 3-76. *Contours over art*

Now this time, let's try something different and use the function **fill-convex-poly** from the core opencv package.

It's not very different from draw-contours, and we indeed just loop on the list and use fill-convex-poly on each of the contours.

```
(def drawing (u/mat-from shapes2))
(set-to drawing rgb/white)

(let[ contours (new-arraylist)]
    (find-contours thresh contours (new-mat) RETR_LIST CHAIN_
    APPROX_SIMPLE)
  (doseq [c contours]
    (fill-convex-poly drawing c rgb/blue-3- LINE_4 1)))
```

And so, we get the four shapes turned to blue (Figure 3-77).

Figure 3-77. *Piece of art turned to blue*

As we can see, the contours and shapes are found and can be drawn.

Another way to draw the contours is to use the function **polylines**. Luckily, the function **polylines** hides the loop over each element of the contours, and you can just pass in as parameters the contour list as is.

```
(set-to drawing rgb/white)

(let[ contours (new-arraylist)]
    (find-contours
            thresh
            contours
            (new-mat)
```

```
        RETR_LIST
        CHAIN_APPROX_SIMPLE)
    (polylines drawing contours true rgb/magenta-2))

(-> drawing clone (u/resize-by 0.5) u/mat-view)
```

And this time, we nicely get the wireframe only of the contours (Figure 3-78).

Figure 3-78. *Wireframe of art*

Alright, but again those shapes for now all have too many points.

Let's again use the approx function that was created, and enhance it so we can specify the factor used by approx-poly-dp.

```
(defn approx_
  ([c] (approx_ c 0.02))
  ([c factor]
  (let[m2f (new-matofpoint2f (.toArray c))
       len (arc-length m2f true)
       ret (new-matofpoint2f)]
    (approx-poly-dp m2f ret (* factor len) true)
    (new-matofpoint (.toArray ret)))))
```

A higher factor means we force the reduction of points to a greater extent. And so, to that effect, let's increase the usual value of 0.02 to 0.03.

```
(set-to drawing rgb/white)

(let[ contours (new-arraylist)]
    (find-contours thresh contours (new-mat) RETR_LIST CHAIN_
    APPROX_SIMPLE)
  (doseq [c contours]
  (fill-convex-poly drawing
                    (approx_ c 0.03)
                    (which-color c) LINE_AA 1)))
```

The shapes have been greatly simplified, and the number of sides has quite diminished: the shapes are now easier to identify (Figure 3-79).

Figure 3-79. *Art with simpler shapes*

3-8 Moving Shapes

Problem

This is based on a problem found on stack overflow.

https://stackoverflow.com/questions/32590277/move-area-of-an-image-to-the-center-using-opencv

The problem was "Move area of an image to the center," with the base picture shown in Figure 3-80.

Figure 3-80. *Moving shapes*

The goal is to move the yellow shape and the black mark inside to the center of the mat.

Solution

I like this recipe quite a lot, because it brings in a lot of origami functions working together toward one goal, which is also the main theme of this chapter.

The plan to achieve our goal is as follows:

- First, add borders to the original picture to see the boundaries

- Switch to the HSV color space

- Create a mask by selecting only the color in-range for yellow

- Create a submat in the original picture from the bounding rect of the preceding mask

- Create the target result mat, of the same size as the original

- Create a submat in the target mat, to the place the content. That submat must be of same size, and it will be located in the center.

- Set the rest of the target mat to any color ...

- We're done!

Let's get started.

How it works

Alright, so the first step was to highlight the border of the mat, because we could not really see up to where it was extending.

We will start by loading the picture and adding borders at the same time.

```
(def img
  (-> "resources/morph/cjy6M.jpg"
      (imread IMREAD_REDUCED_COLOR_2)
      (copy-make-border! 1 1 1 1 BORDER_CONSTANT (->scalar
      "#aabbcc"))))
```

Bordered input with the rounded yellow mark is now shown in Figure 3-81.

Figure 3-81. *Yellow mark and borders*

We then switch to hsv color space and create a mask on the yellow mark, and this is where Origami pipelines make it so much easier to pipe the functions one after the other.

```
(def mask-on-yellow
  (->
    img
    (clone)
    (cvt-color! COLOR_BGR2HSV)
    (in-range! (new-scalar 20 100 100) (new-scalar 30 255 255))))
```

Our yellow mask is ready (Figure 3-82).

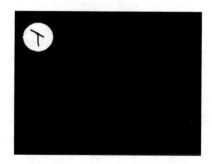

Figure 3-82. *Mask on yellow mark*

Next is to find the contours in the newly created mask mat. Note here the usage of RETR_EXTERNAL, meaning we are only interested in external contours, and so the lines inside the yellow mark will not be included in the returned contour list.

```
(def contours (new-arraylist))
(find-contours mask-on-yellow contours (new-mat) RETR_EXTERNAL
CHAIN_APPROX_SIMPLE)
```

Let's now create an item mat, a submat of the original picture, where the rectangle defining it is made from the bounding rect of the contours.

```
(def background-color  (->scalar "#000000"))
; mask type CV_8UC1 is important !!
(def mask (new-mat (rows img) (cols img) CV_8UC1 background-color))

(def box
  (bounding-rect (first contours)))
(def item
  (submat img box))
```

The item submat is shown in Figure 3-83.

Figure 3-83. *Submat made of the bounding rect of the contour*

We now create a completely new mat, of the same size of the item submat, and copy into the content of the segmented item. The background color has to be the same as the background color of the result mat.

```
(def segmented-item
  (new-mat (rows item) (cols item) CV_8UC3 background-color))

(copy-to item segmented-item (submat mask box) )
```

The newly computed segmented item is shown in Figure 3-84.

Figure 3-84. *Segmented item*

Now let's find the location of the rect that will be the target of the copy. We want the item to be moved to the center, and the rect should be of the same size as the original small box mat.

```
(def center
  (new-point (/ (.cols img ) 2 ) (/ (.rows img) 2)))
(def center-box
  (new-rect
    (- (.-x center ) (/ (.-width box) 2))
    (- (.-y center ) (/ (.-height box) 2))
    (.-width box)
    (.-height box)))
```

Alright, everything is in place; now we create the result mat and copy the content of the segmented item through a copy, via the submat, at the preceding computed centered location.

```
(def result (new-mat (rows img) (cols img) CV_8UC3 background-color))
(def final (submat result center-box))
(copy-to segmented-item final (new-mat))
```

And that's it.

The yellow shape has been moved to the center of a new mat. We made sure the white color of the original mat was not copied over, by specifically using a black background for the final result mat (Figure 3-85).

Figure 3-85. *Victory*

3-9 Looking at Trees

Problem

This is another recipe based on a stack overflow question. The interest this time is to focus on a tree plantation, and before counting the trees, being able to highlight them in an aerial picture.

The referenced question is here:

```
https://stackoverflow.com/questions/31310307/best-way-to-
segment-a-tree-in-plantation-aerial-image-using-opencv
```

Solution

Recognizing the trees will be done with a call to in-range as usual. But the results, as we will see, will still be connected to each other, making it quite hard to actually count anything.

We will introduce the usage of **morphology-ex!** to erode the created mask back and forth, thus making for a better preprocessing mat, ready for counting.

How it works

We will use a picture of a hazy morning forest to work on (Figure 3-86).

Figure 3-86. *Hazy trees*

Eventually, you would want to count the trees, but right now it is even difficult to see them with human eyes. (Any androids around?)

Let's start by creating a mask on the green of the trees.

```
(def in-range-pict
  (-> trees
      clone
      (in-range! (new-scalar 100 80 100) (new-scalar 120 255
      255)) (bitwise-not!)))
```

We get a mask of dots ... as shown in Figure 3-87.

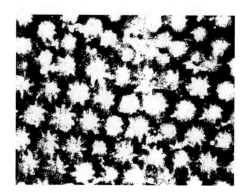

Figure 3-87. *Black and white*

The trick of this recipe comes here. We will apply a MORPH_ERODE followed by a MORPH_OPEN on the in-range-pict mat. This will have the effect of clearing up the forest, and gives each tree its own space.

Morphing is done preparing a mat to pass, as parameter, a kernel matrix created from a small ellipse.

```
(def elem
  (get-structuring-element MORPH_ELLIPSE (new-size 3 3)))
```

If you call **dump** on elem, you will find its internal representation.

```
[0 1 0]
[1 1 1]
[0 1 0]
```

We then use this kernel matrix, by passing it to **morpholy-ex!**.

```
(morphology-ex! in-range-pict MORPH_ERODE elem (new-point -1 -1) 1)
(morphology-ex! in-range-pict MORPH_OPEN elem)
```

This has the desired effect of reducing the size of each tree dot, thus reducing the overlap between the trees (Figure 3-88).

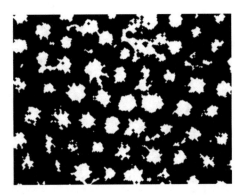

Figure 3-88.   *Trees not overlapping after morph*

To finish, we just apply a simple coloring on the original mat to highlight the position of the trees for the human eye. (Still no androids around?)

```
(def mask
  (->
    in-range-pict
    clone
    (in-range! (new-scalar 0 255 255) (new-scalar 0 0 0))))
```

```
(def target
  (new-mat (.size trees) CV_8UC3))
(set-to target rgb/greenyellow)

(copy-to original target mask)
```

This could be great to do in real time over a video stream.

You also already know what exercise awaits you next. Count the number of trees in the forest by using a quick call to find-contours ...

This is of course left as a free exercise to the reader!

3-10 Detecting Blur
Problem

You have tons of pictures to sort, and you would like to have an automated process to just trash the ones that are blurred.

Solution

The solution is inspired from the pyimagesearch web site entry http://pyimagesearch.com/2015/09/07/blur-detection-with-opencv/, which itself is pointing at the paper **variation of the Laplacian** by Pech-Pacheco et al, "Diatom autofocusing in brightfield microscopy: A comparative study."

It does highlight cool ways of putting OpenCV and here origami into actions quickly for something useful.

Basically, you need to apply a Laplacian filter on the one-channel version of your image. Then, you compute the deviation of the result from the preceding and check if the deviation is below a given threshold.

The filter itself is applied with **filter-2-d!,** while the variance is computed with **mean-std-dev**.

How it works

The Laplacian matrix/kernel to be used for the filter puts emphasis on the center pixel and reduces emphasis on the left/right top/bottom ones.

This is the Laplacian kernel that we are going to use.

```
(def laplacian-kernel
  (u/matrix-to-mat
  [ [ 0 -1  0]
    [-1  4 -1]
    [ 0 -1  0]
  ]))
```

Let's apply this kernel with filter-2-d!, followed by a call to mean-std-dev to compute the median and the deviation.

```
(filter-2-d! img -1 laplacian-kernel)
(def std (new-matofdouble))
(def median (new-matofdouble))
(mean-std-dev img median std)
```

When processing a picture, you can view the results of the averages with dump, since they are matrices. This is shown in the following:

```
(dump median)
; [19.60282552083333]
```

```
(dump std)
; [45.26957788759024]
```

Finally, the value to compare to detect blur will be the deviation raised to the power of 2.

```
(Math/pow (first (.get std 0 0)) 2)
```

We will then get a value that will be compared to 50. Lower than 50 means the image is blurred. Greater than 50 means the image is showing as not blurred.

Let's create an is-image-blurred? function made of all the preceding steps:

```
(defn std-laplacian [img]
  (let [ std (new-matofdouble)]
    (filter-2-d! img -1 laplacian-kernel)
    (mean-std-dev img (new-matofdouble) std)
    (Math/pow (first (.get std 0 0)) 2)))

(defn is-image-blurred?[img]
  (< (std-laplacian (clone img)) 50))
```

Now let's apply that function to a few pictures.

```
(-> "resources/chapter03/cat-bg-blurred.jpg"
    (imread IMREAD_REDUCED_GRAYSCALE_4)
    (is-image-blurred?))
```

And ... our first test passes! The cat of Figure 3-89 indeed gives a deserved blurred result.

Figure 3-89. *Blurred cat*

And what about one of the most beautiful cat on this planet? That worked too. The cat from Figure 3-90 is recognized as sharp!

Figure 3-90. *Sharp but sleepy cat*

Now, probably time to go and sort all your beachside summer pictures… But yes, of course, yes, agreed, not all blurred pictures are to be trashed.

3-11 Making Photomosaics
Problem

In a project lab, now maybe 20 years ago, I saw a gigantic *Star Wars* poster, made of multiple small scenes of the first movie, *A New Hope*.

The poster was huge, and when seen from a bit far away, it was actually a picture of Darth Vader offering his hand to Luke.

The poster left a great impression, and I always wanted to do one of my own. Recently, I also learned there was a name for this type of created picture: photomosaic.

Solution

The concept is way simpler than what I originally thought. Basically, the hardest part is to download the pictures.

You mainly need two inputs, a final picture, and a set of pictures to use as subs.

The work consists of computing the mean average of the RGB channels for each picture, and creating an index from it.

Once this first preparation step is done, create a grid over the picture to be replicated, and then for each cell of the grid, compute the norm between the two averages: the one from the cell, and the one from each file of the index.

Finally, replace the sub of the big picture with the picture from the index that has the lowest mean average, meaning the picture that is visually closer to the submat.

Let's put this in action!

How it works

The first step is to write a function that computes the mean average of the colors of a mat. We use again **mean-std-dev** for that effect, and since we are only interested in the mean for this exercise, this is the result returned by the function.

```
(defn mean-average-bgr [mat]
  (let [_mean (new-matofdouble)]
    (-> mat clone
    (median-blur! 3)
    (mean-std-dev _mean (new-matofdouble)))
    _mean))
```

Let's call this on any picture to see what happens.

```
(-> "resources/chapter03/emilie1.jpg"
    (imread IMREAD_REDUCED_COLOR_8)
    get-averages-bgr-mat
    dump)
```

273

The return values are shown in the following. Those values are the mean average for each of the three RGB channels.

```
[123.182]
[127.38]
[134.128]
```

Let's sidestep a bit and compare the norms of three matrices: ex1, ex2, and ex3. Looking at their content, you can "feel" that ex1 and ex2 are closer than ex1 and ex3.

```
(def ex1 (u/matrix-to-mat [[0 1 2]]))
(def ex2 (u/matrix-to-mat [[0 1 3]]))
(def ex3 (u/matrix-to-mat [[0 1 7]]))

(norm ex1 ex2)
; 1.0
(norm ex1 ex3)
; 5.0
```

This is confirmed by the result of the output of the norm function, which calculates the distance between the matrices.

And this is what we are going to use. First, we create an index of all the files available. The index is a map created by loading each image as a mat, and computing its mean-average-bgr.

```
(defn indexing [files for-size]
  (zipmap files
      (map #(-> % imread (resize! for-size) mean-average-bgr)
      files)))
```

The output of the function is a map where each element is a set of key,val like filepath -> mean-average-bgr.

To find the closest image now that we have an index, we compute the norm of the mat (or submat later on) considered, and all the possible mean-bgr matrices of our index.

We then sort and take the lowest possible value. This is what find-closest does.

```
(defn find-closest [ target indexed ]
  (let [mean-bgr-target (get-averages-bgr-mat target)]
    (first
      (sort-by val <
        (apply-to-vals indexed #(norm mean-bgr-target %))))))
```

apply-to-vals is a function that takes a hashmap and a function, applies a function to all the values in the map, and leaves the rest as is.

```
(defn apply-to-vals [m f]
  (into {} (for [[k v] m] [k (f v)])))
```

The hardest part is done; let's get to the meat of the photomosaic algorithm.

The tile function is a function that creates a grid of the input picture and retrieves submats, one for each tile of the grid.

It then loops over all the submats one by one, computes the submat's mean color average using the same function, and then calls **find-closest** with that average and the previously created index.

The call to **find-closest** returns a file path, which we load a submat from and then replace the tile's submat in the target picture, just by copying the loaded mat with the usual **copy-to**.

See this in the function tile written here.

```
(defn tile [org indexed ^long grid-x ^long grid-y]
  (let[
    dst (u/mat-from org)
    width (/ (.cols dst) grid-x)
```

```
height (/ (.rows dst) grid-y)
total (* grid-x grid-y)
cache (java.util.HashMap.)
]
(doseq [^long i (range 0 grid-y)]
  (doseq [^long j (range 0 grid-x)]
  (let [
    square
     (submat org (new-rect (* j width) (* i height) width
     height ))
    best (first (find-closest square indexed))
    img  (get-cache-image cache best  width height)
    sub (submat dst (new-rect (* j width) (* i height)
    width height ))
    ]
     (copy-to img sub))))
dst))
```

The main entry point is a function named **photomosaic**, which calls the tile algorithm by just creating the index of averages upfront, and passing it to the **tile** function.

```
(defn photomosaic
  [images-folder target-image output grid-x grid-y ]
  (let [files    (collect-pictures images-folder)
        indexed (indexing (collect-pictures images-folder)
        (new-size grid-x grid-y))
        target   (imread target-image )]
    (tile target indexed grid-x grid-y)))
```

Whoo-hoo. It's all there. Creating the photomosaic is now as simple as calling the function of the same name with the proper parameters:

- Folder of jpg images

- The picture we want to mosaic

- The size of the grid

Here is a simple sample:

```
(def lechat
  (photomosaic
    "resources/cat_photos"
    "resources/chapter03/emilie5.jpg"
    100 100))
```

And the first photomosaic ever of Marcel the cat is shown in Figure 3-91.

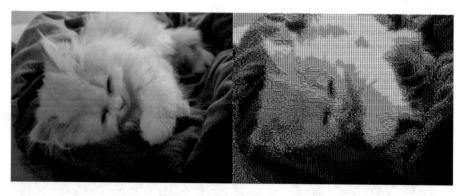

Figure 3-91. *Mosaic of a sleeping cat*

Another photomosaic input/output, this from Kenji's cat, is in Figure 3-92.

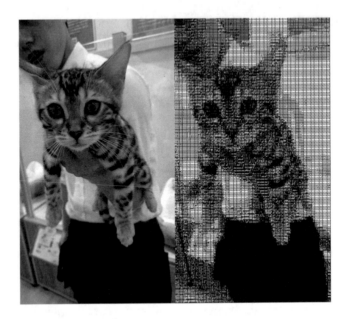

Figure 3-92. *Kogure-san's cat*

And, a romantic mosaic in Figure 3-93.

Figure 3-93. *Neko from Fukuoka*

Cats used in the pictures are all included in the examples, not a single cat has been harmed, and so now is probably your turn to create your own awesome-looking mosaics... Enjoy!

CHAPTER 4

Real-Time Video

"IF A
PICTURE IS
WORTH A
THOUSAND
WORDS,
WHAT'S
A VIDEO
WORTH?"

Up to now, this book has been focused on getting the reader up to speed with working on images and generated graphical art. You should now feel pretty confident with the methods introduced, and you have room for many ideas.

Great!

We could keep going on expanding and explaining more on the other methods from OpenCV, but we are going to do something else in Chapter 4, as we switch to real-time video analysis, applying the knowledge learned during the previous chapters to the field of video streaming.

© Nicolas Modrzyk 2018
N. Modrzyk, *Java Image Processing Recipes*, https://doi.org/10.1007/978-1-4842-3465-5_4

You may ask: What is real-time video analysis and why would I do that? OpenCV makes it a breeze to look into video streams and focus on the content of the video. For example, how many people are there showing on a video stream now? Are there cats in this video? Is this a tennis game, and the root of all questions, is it a sunny day today?

OpenCV has many of those algorithms implemented for you, and what's even better, Origami adds a bit of sweet sugar, so you can get started straightaway and put blocks together in an easy way.

In this chapter, we will get started with a first recipe that will show you how little is required to be ready for video streaming.

Then, we move on to more substantial subjects like face recognition, background diffing, and finding oranges and most importantly, body soap.

4-1 Getting Started with Video Streaming

Problem

You have the Origami setup for image processing; now, you would like to know the origami setup for video processing.

Solution

Well, the bad news is that there is no extra project setup. So, we could almost close this recipe already.

The good news is that there are two functions that Origami gives you, but before using them we will cover how the underlying processing works.

First, we will create a **videocapture** object from the origami opencv3. video package and start/stop a stream with it.

Second, since we think this should definitely be easier to use, we will introduce the function that does everything for you: **u/simple-cam-window**.

Last, we will review **u/cams-window,** which makes it easy to combine multiple streams from different sources.

How it works

Do-It-Yourself Video Stream

You could skip this small section of the recipe, but it's actually quite informative to know what is behind the scenes.

The simple idea of video stream manipulation starts with creating an opencv videocapture object that accesses available video devices.

That object can then return you a mat object, just like all the mat objects you have used so far. It is possible to then act on the mat object, and in the simplest case show the mat in a frame on the screen.

Origami uses something similar to **u/imshow** to display mats taken from video, but for this very first example let's simply use u/imshow to display the mat.

Here, we do require another namespace: **[opencv3.video :as v]**, but later on you will see that this step is not necessary, and you would require that extra video namespace only when using opencv video functions directly.

Let's see how it goes by going through the following code example.

First, we create the videocapture object, which can access all the webcams of your host system.

We then open the camera with ID 0. That is probably the default in your environment, but we will also see later how to play with multiple devices.

```
(def capture (v/new-videocapture))
(.open capture 0)
```

We need a window to display the frame recorded from the device, and sure enough, we'll create a binding named window. This window will be set to have a black background.

```
(def window
 (u/show (new-mat 200 200 CV_8UC3 rgb/black)))
```

We then create a buffer to receive video data, as a regular OpenCV mat.

```
(def buffer (new-mat))
```

The core video loop will copy content to the buffer mat using the **read** function on the capture object, and then it will show the buffer in the window, using the function **u/re-show**.

```
(dotimes [_ 100]
  (.read capture buffer)
  (u/re-show window buffer))
```

At this stage, you should see frames showing up in a window on your screen, as in Figure 4-1.

Figure 4-1. *My favorite body soap*

Finally, when the loop has finished, the webcam is released using the **release** function on the capture object.

```
(.release capture)
```

This should also have the effect of turning off the camera LED of your computer. One thing to think about at the end of this small exercise is ... yes, this is a standard mat object that was used as a buffer in the display loop, and so, yes, you could already plug in some text or color conversion before displaying it.

One-Function Webcam

Now that you understand how the underlying webcam handling is done, here is another slightly shorter way of getting you to the same result, using **u/simple-cam-window**.

In this small section, we want to quickly review how to take the stream and manipulate it using that function.

In its simplest form, simple-cam-window is used with the identity function as the parameter. As you remember, identity takes an element and returns it as is.

```
(u/simple-cam-window identity)
```

Providing you have a webcam connected, this will start the same streaming video with the content of the stream showing in a frame.

The function takes a single parameter, which is the function applied to the mat before it is shown inside the frame.

Sweet. We'll get back to it in a few seconds, but for now, here's what you'll find: simply converting the recording frames to a different colormap, you could pass an anonymous function only using **apply-color-map!**.

```
(u/simple-cam-window #(apply-color-map! % COLORMAP_HOT))
```

With the immediate result showing in Figure 4-2.

Figure 4-2. *Hot body soap*

In the second version of **u/simple-cam-window**, you can specify settings for the frame and the video recording, all of this as a simple map passed as the first parameter to simple-cam-window.

For example:

```
(u/simple-cam-window
{:frame {:color "#ffcc88", :title "video", :width 350,
 :height 300}
  :video {:device 0, :width 100, :height 120}}
  identity)
```

In the map, the video key specifies the device ID, the device to take stream from, and the size of the frame to record. Note that if the size is not according to what the device is capable of, the setting will be silently ignored.

In the same parameter map, the frame key can specify the parameter, as seen in previous chapter, with the background color, the title, and the size of the window.

Ok, great; all set with the basics. Let's play a bit.

Transformation Function

The identity function takes an element and returns it as is. We saw how identity worked in the first cam usage, by returning the mat as it was recorded by the opencv framework.

Now, say you would like to write a function that

- takes a mat

- resizes the mat by a factor of 0.5

- changes the color map to WINTER

- adds the current date as a white overlay

Not so difficult with all the knowledge you have gathered so far. Let's write a small origami pipeline in a function **my-fn!** to do the image transformation:

```
(defn my-fn! [mat]
  (-> mat
    (u/resize-by 0.5)
    (apply-color-map! COLORMAP_WINTER)
    (put-text! (str (java.util.Date.)) (new-point 10 50) FONT_
HERSHEY_PLAIN 1 rgb/white 1)  ))
```

Note here that the pipeline returns the transformed mat. Now let's use this newly created pipeline on a still image.

```
(-> "resources/chapter03/ai5.jpg"
    imread
    my-fn!
    u/mat-view)
```

And let's enjoy a simple winter feline output (Figure 4-3).

Figure 4-3. *Cool feline*

And then, if you are in Starbucks and using your laptop webcam, you can use the new function my-fn! straight onto a video stream by passing it as an argument to simple-cam-window.

```
(u/simple-cam-window my-fn!)
```

Which would give you something like Figure 4-4.

Figure 4-4. *Starbucks ice coffee refill*

Two Frames, or More, from the Same Input Source

This is a convenient method when trying to apply two or more functions from the same source. This is really only a matter of using the clone function to avoid memory conflicts with the source buffer.

Here, we create a function that takes the buffer as input, and then concatenates two images created from the same buffer. The first image on the left will be a black-and-white version of the stream, while the right one will be a flipped version of the buffer.

```
(u/simple-cam-window
   (fn [buffer]
   (vconcat! [
    (-> buffer
        clone
        (cvt-color! COLOR_RGB2GRAY)
        (cvt-color! COLOR_GRAY2RGB))
    (-> buffer clone (flip! -1)) ])))
```

Note that we use the clone twice for each side of the concatenation (Figure 4-5).

Figure 4-5. *Gray left, flipped right, but it is still body soap*

287

You can push this method even further by cloning the input buffer as many times as you want; to highlight this, here is another example of applying a different color map three times onto the same input buffer.

```
(u/simple-cam-window
    (fn [buffer]
    (hconcat! [
      (-> buffer clone (apply-color-map! COLORMAP_JET))
      (-> buffer clone (apply-color-map! COLORMAP_BONE))
      (-> buffer clone (apply-color-map! COLORMAP_PARULA))]))))
```

And the result is shown in Figure 4-6.

Figure 4-6. *Jet, bone, and parula, but this is still body soap*

4-2 Combining Multiple Video Streams

Problem

You played around creating many outputs from the same buffer, but it would be nice to also be able to plug in multiple cameras and combine their buffers together.

Solution

Origami comes with a sibling function to u/simple-cam-window named **u/cams-window,** which is an enhanced version where you can combine multiple streams from the same or multiple sources.

How it works

u/cams-window is a function that takes a list of devices, each defining a device from an ID, and usually a transformation function.

The function also takes a video function to concatenate two or more device outputs, and finally a frame element to define the usual parameters of the window, like sizes and title.

```
(u/cams-window
   {:devices [
     {:device 0 :width 300 :height 200 :fn identity}
     {:device 1 :width 300 :height 200 :fn identity}]
    :video { :fn
              #(hconcat! [
                 (-> %1 (resize! (new-size 300 200)))
                 (-> %2 (resize! (new-size 300 200))) ])}
    :frame
    {:width 650 :height 250 :title "OneOfTheSame"}})
```

Figure 4-7 shows two devices targeting the same body soap, but from different angles.

The left frame takes input from the device with ID 0, and the right frame input from the device with ID 1.

Figure 4-7. *More body soap pictures*

Note that even though sizes are specified for each device, a resize is actually still needed, because devices have very specific combinations of height and width they can use, and so using different devices may be a bit of a challenge.

Still, the resize! call in the combining video function does not feel out of place, and things work smoothly afterward.

4-3 Warping Video

Problem

This recipe is about warping the buffer of the video stream using a transformation, but it is also about updating the transformation in real time.

Solution

The warping transformation itself will be done using opencv's **get-perspective-transform** from the core namespace.

The real-time updating will be done using a Clojure atom, with the software transactional memory, well suited here to update the value of the matrix required to do the transformation, while the display loop is reading the content of that matrix, thus always getting the latest value.

How it works

To perform a perspective transform, we need a warp matrix. The warp matrix is contained in an atom and first initialized to nil.

```
(def mt
  (atom nil))
```

The warp matrix used to do the transformation can be created from four points, with their locations before and after the transformation.

Instead of acting on a local binding, we will update the atom value using **reset!**.

```
(def points1
  [[100 10]
   [200 100]
   [28 200]
   [389 390]])
```

```
(def points2
  [[70 10]
   [200 140]
   [20 200]
   [389 390]])
```

```
(reset! mt
  (get-perspective-transform
   (u/matrix-to-matofpoint2f points1)
   (u/matrix-to-matofpoint2f points2)))
```

Remember, you can still dump the warp matrix, which is a regular 3×3 mat, by using a dereferencing call on it, using @, or **deref**.

```
(dump @mt)
```

With the points defined in the preceding, this gives the following matrix of doubles.

```
[1.789337561985906 0.3234215275201738 -94.5799621372129]
[0.7803091692375479 1.293303360247406 -78.45137776386103]
[0.002543030309135725 -3.045754676722361E-4 1]
```

Now let's create the function that will warp a mat using the matrix saved in the mt atom.

```
(defn warp! [ buffer ]
  (-> buffer
    (warp-perspective! @mt (size buffer ))))
```

Remember that this function can still be applied to standard images; for example, if you want to warp cats, you could write the following origami pipeline:

```
(-> "resources/chapter03/ai5.jpg"
    imread
    (u/resize-by 0.7)
    warp!
    u/imshow)
```

And the two cats from before would be warping as in Figure 4-8.

Figure 4-8. *Warped cats*

Now let's apply that function to a video stream, using **warp!** as a parameter to the u/simple-cam window.

```
(u/simple-cam-window warp!)
```

The body soap has been warped! (Figure 4-9)

Obviously, the book is not doing too much to express the difference between a still cat image and the body soap stream, so you can plug in your own stream there.

Figure 4-9. *Warped body soap*

4-4 Using Face Recognition

Problem

While the OpenCV face recognition features work perfectly fine on still pictures, working on video streams differs in terms of looking for moving faces showing up in real time, as well as counting people and so on.

Solution

The first step is to load a classifier: the opencv object that will be able to find out the matching element on a mat.

The classifier is loaded from an xml definition using the origami function **new-cascadeclassifier**.

Then, a call to **detectMultiScale** with that classifier and a mat will return a list of matching rect objects.

Those rect objects can then be used to highlight the found faces with a rectangle, or for creating submat.

How it works

There is no extra Clojure namespace required to make this work, as the new-cascadeclassifier function is already in the core namespace.

If the xml file is on the file system, then you can load the classifier with

```
(def detector
  (new-cascadeclassifier
    "resources/lbpcascade_frontalface.xml"))
```

If the xml is stored as a resource in a jar file, then you could load it with

```
(def detector
  (new-cascadeclassifier
    (.getPath (clojure.java.io/resource "lbpcascade_
frontalface.xml"))))
```

Rectangle objects found by the classifier will need to be drawn. The classifier's detect function returns a list of rectangles, so let's write a function that simply loops over the list of rect objects and draws a blue line border on each rect.

```
(defn draw-rects! [buffer rects]
  (doseq [rect (.toArray rects)]
    (rectangle
    buffer
    (new-point (.-x rect) (.-y rect))
    (new-point (+ (.-width rect) (.-x rect)) (+ (.-height rect)
    (.-y rect)))
```

```
rgb/blue
5))
buffer)
```

Then let's define a second function, **find-faces!,** which calls the detectMultiScale method on the classifier and draws the rectangles using the draw-rects! function defined in the preceding.

```
(defn find-faces![buffer]
  (let [rects (new-matofrect)]
    (.detectMultiScale detector buffer rects)
    (-> buffer
        (draw-rects! rects)
        (u/resize-by 0.7))))
```

We have all the blocks here again, and it's now a simple matter of calling **find-faces!** through **u/simple-cam-window**.

```
(u/simple-cam-window find-faces!)
```

And if you find yourself in Starbucks one morning on a terrace, the image could be something like Figure 4-10.

Figure 4-10. *Quiet impressive morning coffee face*

The draw-rects! function could really be anything since you have access to a buffer object.

For example, this second version of **draw-rects!** applies a different color map on the submat created by the rect of the found face.

```
(defn draw-rects! [buffer rects]
   (doseq [r (.toArray rects)]
     (-> buffer
      (submat r)
      (apply-color-map! COLORMAP_COOL)
      (copy-to (submat buffer r))))
     (put-text! buffer (str (count (.toArray rects) ) )
      (new-point 30 100) FONT_HERSHEY_PLAIN 5 rgb/magenta-2 2))
```

And reusing the created building blocks, this gives the cool face from Figure 4-11.

Figure 4-11. *Cool morning coffee face*

This last example of drawing faces takes the first found face and makes a big close-up on the right-hand side of the video stream.

```
(defn draw-rects! [buffer rects]
  (if (> (count (.toArray rects)) 0)
```

```
(let [r (first (.toArray rects))
      s (-> buffer clone (submat r) (resize! (.size
      buffer)))]
      (hconcat! [buffer s]))
   buffer))
```

Obviously, Figure 4-12 will quickly get you convinced that this should really only be used for house BBQs, in order to show everyone who has been eating all the meat.

Figure 4-12. *Overview and close-up on the same video window*

4-5 Diffing with a Base Image

Problem

You would like to take a mat image, define it as a base, and discover changes made to that base image.

Solution

This is a very short recipe but is quite helpful on its own to understand the more complex recipe on movement that is coming after.

To create a diff of an image and its base, we here first create two pieces of video callback code: one will store the background picture in a Clojure atom, and the other will do a diff with that base atom.

A grayed version of the result will then be passed through a simple threshold function, to prepare the result for additional shape recognition and/or for further processing.

How it works

To compute a diff of an image with another one, you need two mats: one for the base, and one updated version with (we hope) new extra shapes in it.

We start by defining the Clojure atom and starting a video stream to create an atom with a reference on the image of the background.

As long as the cam-window is running, the latest buffer mat from the video stream will be stored in the atom.

```
(def base-image (atom nil))

(u/simple-cam-window
  (fn [buffer] (swap! base-image (fn[_] buffer) ) ))
```

Once you are happy enough with the background, you can stop the cam-window and check the currently stored background for the picture with imshow and a deref-ed version of the atom.

```
(u/imshow @base-image)
```

This time, the image is a typical one of a busy home workplace (Figure 4-13).

Figure 4-13. *Hearts and a speaker*

Now, the next step is to define a new stream callback to use with simple-cam-window, which will diff with the mat stored in the Clojure atom.

The diff is done with the opencv function **absdiff**, which takes three mats, namely, the two inputs to diff and the output.

```
(defn diff-with-bg [buffer]
   (let[ output (new-mat)]
     (absdiff buffer @base-image output)
     output))

(u/simple-cam-window diff-with-bg)
```

Obviously, before starting the second stream and introducing new shapes, you should stop the first recording stream.

This would give something like Figure 4-14, where the added body soap is clearly being recognized.

Figure 4-14. *Body soap in the office!*

Now usually, the next step is to clean the shape showing on top of the background a bit by turning the diff mat to gray and applying a very high threshold after a blur.

```
; diff in gray
(defn diff-in-gray [buffer]
 (-> buffer
  clone
  (cvt-color! COLOR_RGB2GRAY)
  (median-blur! 7)
  (threshold! 10 255 1)))
```

We have two processing functions for the same buffer, and in Clojure it is actually quite easy to combine them with **comp**, so let's try this now.

Remember that **comp** combines the function from right to left, meaning the first function that is being applied is the rightmost one.

```
(u/simple-cam-window (comp diff-in-gray diff-with-bg ))
```

See the composition result and the shape of the body soap showing in Figure 4-15.

Figure 4-15. *Added shape worked for more processing*

Here, you could compile all the steps, creating a simple mask from the preceding added shape mat, and use the mask to highlight the diff-ed part only.

None of this is too surprising, except maybe the bitwise-not! call, summarized in the highlight-new! function.

```
(defn highlight-new! [buffer]
 (let [output (u/mat-from buffer) w (-> buffer
   clone
   diff-with-bg
   (cvt-color! COLOR_RGB2GRAY)
   (median-blur! 7)
   (threshold! 10 255 1)
   (bitwise-not!))]
 (set-to output rgb/black)
 (copy-to buffer output w)
 output))
```

And the body soap output shows in Figure 4-16.

Figure 4-16. *Back to body soap*

The streams were taken during a heavy jet lag around 3 am, and so the lighting conditions give a bit of noise at the bottom of the body soap, but you could try to remove that noise by updating the mask to not include the desk wood color. Your turn!

4-6 Finding Movement

Problem

You would like to identify and highlight movement and moving shapes in a video stream.

Solution

We start by doing an accumulation of the float values of the buffer, after cleaning it up. This is done with the function **accumulate-weighted**.

Then, we do a diff between the grayed version of the buffer and the computed average mat, and we retrieve a mask mat of the delta as quickly presented in the previous recipe.

Finally, we apply a threshold on the delta, clean up the result with a bit of dilation, and transform the mat back to color mode to be displayed onscreen.

This is actually easier than it sounds!

How it works

Here, we would like to show on a mat the delta created by the movements.

Finding Movement in Black and White

The first step is to take a buffer and create a cleaned (via a blur) gray version of it.

We are not interested to display this mat, but just to perform arithmetic on it; we will convert the mat to a 32-bit float mat, or in opencv language **CV_32F**.

```
(defn gray-clean! [buffer]
  (-> buffer
      clone
      (cvt-color! COLOR_BGR2GRAY)
      (gaussian-blur! (new-size 3 3) 0)
      (convert-to! CV_32F)))
```

This function will be used to prepare a gray version of the mat. Let's now work on computing the accumulated average and a diff between the average and the most recent buffer.

We'll create another function, **find-movement**, which will highlight, in black and white, recent movement in the picture.

That function will get a Clojure atom, **avg**, as a parameter to keep track of the average value of the video's incoming mat objects. The second parameter is the usual buffer mat passed to the callback. The function will display the frame-delta.

In the first if switch, we make sure the average mat, stored in the atom, is initialized with a proper value from the incoming stream.

Then a diff is computed using absdiff, onto which we apply a short threshold-dilate-cvt-color pipeline to show the movements directly.

```
(defn find-movement [ avg buffer]
  (let [gray (gray-clean! buffer) frame-delta (new-mat)]

    (if (nil? @avg)
     (reset! avg gray))

    ; compute the absolute diff on the weighted average
    (accumulate-weighted gray @avg 0.05 (new-mat))
    (absdiff gray @avg frame-delta)

    ; apply threshold and convert back to RGB for display
    (-> frame-delta
     (threshold! 35 255 THRESH_BINARY)
     (dilate! (new-mat))
     (cvt-color! COLOR_GRAY2RGB)
     (u/resize-by 0.8))))
```

We finally define a function wrapping the find-movement function, with an inlined Clojure atom. That atom will contain the average of the mat objects.

```
(def find-movements!
  (partial find-movement (atom nil)))
```

Time to put those functions in action with u/simple-cam-window.

```
(u/simple-cam-window find-movements!)
```

This is shown in Figure 4-17.

Figure 4-17. *Movement is detected!*

We would like to show movements here, but because the amount of black ink required to print this is going to scare the publisher, let's add a bitwise operation to do a black-on-white instead and see how the live progression goes.

Let's update the find-movement function with a bitwise-not! call on the frame-delta mat. Before that, we need to convert the matrix back to something we can work on, using opencv's convert-to! function, with a type target CV_8UC3, which is usually what we work with.

```
(defn find-movement [ avg buffer]
  (let [gray (gray-clean! buffer) frame-delta (new-mat)]
    ...

  (-> frame-delta
    (threshold! 35 255 THRESH_BINARY)
    (dilate! (new-mat))
    (convert-to! CV_8UC3)
    (bitwise-not!)
    (cvt-color! COLOR_GRAY2RGB)
    (u/resize-by 0.8))))
```

Good; let's call simple-cam again. Wow. Figure 4-18 now looks a bit scary.

Figure 4-18. *Scary black-on-white movement*

And if you stop getting agitated in front of your computer, the movement highlights are stabilizing and slowly moving to a fully white mat, as shown in the progression of Figure 4-19.

Figure 4-19. *Stabilizing movement*

Find and Draw Contours

At this stage, it would be easy to find and draw contours to highlight movement on the original colored buffer.

Let's find contours of the nice movement mat that you managed to create.

A few more lines are added to the find-movement function, notably the finding contours on the delta mat and the drawing on the color mat.

You have seen all of this find-contours dance in the previous chapter, so let's get down to the updated code.

```
(defn find-movement [ avg buffer]
  (let [ gray (base-gray! buffer)
         frame-delta (new-mat)
         contours (new-arraylist)]

    (if (nil? @avg)
      (reset! avg gray))

    (accumulate-weighted gray @avg 0.05 (new-mat))
    (absdiff gray @avg frame-delta)

    (-> frame-delta
     (threshold! 35 255 THRESH_BINARY)
     (dilate! (new-mat))
     (convert-to! CV_8UC3)
     (find-contours contours (new-mat) RETR_EXTERNAL CHAIN_
     APPROX_SIMPLE))

    (-> frame-delta
     (bitwise-not!)
     (cvt-color! COLOR_GRAY2RGB)
     (u/resize-by 0.8))

    (-> buffer
     ; (u/draw-contours-with-rect! contours )
     (u/draw-contours-with-line! contours)
     (u/resize-by 0.8))

    (hconcat! [frame-delta buffer]) ))
```

Calling this new version of the find-movement function gives
something like Figure 4-20, but you can probably be way more creative
from there.

Figure 4-20. *Highlights moving parts in blue*

4-7 Separating the Foreground from the Background Using Grabcut

Problem

Grabcut is another opencv method that can be used to separate the
foreground from the background of an image. But can it be used in real
time like on a video stream?

Solution

There is indeed a grab-cut function that easily separates the front from
the background. The function needs just a bit of understanding to see the
different masks required to get it going, so we will focus first on understanding
how things works on a still image.

We will then move on to the live stream solution. This will quickly
lead to a speed problem, because grab-cut takes more time than what is
available with real-time processing.

So, we will use a small trick by turning down the resolution of the work area just to bring the time used by grab-cut to a minimum; then, we'll use the full resolution when performing the rest of the processing, resulting in a grabcut.

How it works

On a Still Image

Here we want to call grabcut and separate a *depth* layer from the other ones.

The idea with grabcut is to prepare to use either a rectangle or a mask on the input picture and pass it to the grabcut function.

The result stored in that single output mask will contain a set of 1.0, 2.0, or 3.0 scalar values depending on what grabcut thinks is part of each of the different layers.

Then we use opencv **compare** on this mask and another fixed 1×1 mat of the scalar value of the layer we would like to retrieve. We obtain a mask only for the layer of interest.

Finally, we do a copy of the original image, on an output mat, using the mask created in step 2.

Ready? Let's go for a cat example.

First, we load one of those cat pictures that we love so much and turn it to a proper working-size mat object.

```
(def source "resources/chapter03/ai6.jpg")
(def img (-> source imread (u/resize-by 0.5)))
```

The loaded cat picture is shown in Figure 4-21.

Figure 4-21. *A feline kiss for you*

Then, we define a **mask** mat, which will receive the output of the grabcut call, namely, per-pixel information about the layer info.

We also define a rectangle for the region of interest (ROI) of where we want the grabcut to be done, here almost the full picture, mostly just removing the borders.

```
(def mask (new-mat))
(def rect
  (new-rect
    (new-point 10 10)
    (new-size (- (.width img) 30) (- (.height img) 30 ))))
```

Now that we have all the required inputs for grabcut, let's call it with the mask, the ROI, and the **grabcut init param**, here GC_INIT_WITH_RECT. The other available method is to use **GC_INIT_WITH_MASK**, which as you probably have guessed is initialized with a mask instead of a rect.

```
(grab-cut img mask rect (new-mat) (new-mat) 11 GC_INIT_WITH_RECT)
```

Grabcut has been called. To get an idea of the retrieved content of the output, let's quickly see the matrix content on a small submat of the mask.

```
(dump (submat mask (new-rect (new-point 10 10) (new-size 5 5))))
```

If you try it yourself, you would see values like

```
[2 2 2 2 2]
[2 2 2 2 2]
[2 2 2 2 2]
[2 2 2 2 2]
[2 2 2 2 2]
```

Another submat dump elsewhere in the mat gives a different result:

```
(dump (submat mask (new-rect (new-point 150 150) (new-size 5 5))))
```

In turn, this gives

```
[3 3 3 3 3]
[3 3 3 3 3]
[3 3 3 3 3]
[3 3 3 3 3]
[3 3 3 3 3]
```

We can guess from this different matrix that the layer is different.

The idea here is to retrieve a mask made of all the same values, so now let's create a mask from all the pixels that are contained in layer 3, meaning that they are made of 3.0 values.

We'll call this the fg-mask, for foreground mask.

```
(def fg-mask (clone mask))
(def source1 (new-mat 1 1 CV_8U (new-scalar 3.0)))
(compare mask source1 fg-mask CMP_EQ)
(u/mat-view fg-mask)
```

The cat foreground mask is shown in Figure 4-22.

Figure 4-22. *Foreground mask*

We can then use copy-to from the original input image, and the fg-mask on a new black mat of the same size as the input.

```
(def fg_foreground (-> img (u/mat-from)  (set-to rgb/black)))
(copy-to img fg_foreground fg-mask)
(u/mat-view fg_foreground)
```

And we get the mat of Figure 4-23.

Figure 4-23. *Only the foreground of the feline kiss*

Notice how we get a bit of an approximation where the two kittens cross each other, but overall the result is pretty effective.

Before moving on, let's quickly retrieve the complementary mask, the background mask, by focusing on the layer with scalar values of 2.0.

First, we create a mask again to receive the output, this time **bg-mask**.

```
(def bg-mask (clone mask))
(def source2 (new-mat 1 1 CV_8U (new-scalar 2.0)))
(compare mask source2 bg-mask CMP_EQ)
(u/mat-view bg-mask)
```

The result for the background mask is shown in Figure 4-24.

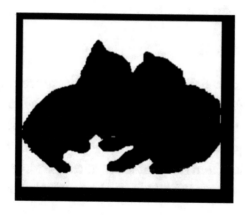

Figure 4-24. *Background mask*

Then, simply do a copy similar to the one that was done for the foreground.

```
(def bg_foreground (-> img (u/mat-from)  (set-to (new-scalar 0
0 0))))
(copy-to img bg_foreground bg-mask)
(u/mat-view bg_foreground)
```

And the result is shown in Figure 4-25.

Figure 4-25. *Mat of the background layer*

Now that you have seen how to separate the different layers on a still image, let's move on to video streaming.

On a Video Stream

As you may have noticed, the grabcut step in the preceding example was very slow, mostly due to a lot of heavy computations done to achieve a clean separation of the different layers. But how bad is it?

Let's give it a quick try with a first dumb version of a real-time grabcut.

We'll call this function **in-front-slow**, and basically just compile the steps we have just seen in the still example in a single function.

```
(defn in-front-slow [buffer]
  (let [
        img (clone buffer)
        rect (new-rect
          (new-point 5 5)
          (new-size (- (.width buffer) 5) (- (.height buffer)
          5 )))
        mask (new-mat)
        pfg-mask (new-mat)
        source1 (new-mat 1 1 CV_8U (new-scalar 3.0))
```

```
    pfg_foreground (-> buffer (u/mat-from)  (set-to rgb/
    black))]

(grab-cut img mask rect (new-mat) (new-mat) 7 GC_INIT_WITH_
RECT)
(compare mask source1 pfg-mask CMP_EQ)
(copy-to buffer pfg_foreground pfg-mask)
pfg_foreground))
```

And then, let's use this function as a callback to our now-familiar **u/simple-cam-window**.

```
(u/simple-cam-window in-front-slow)
```

This slowly gives the output seen in Figure 4-26.

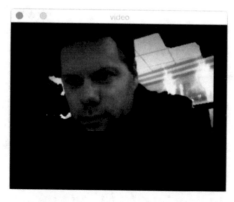

Figure 4-26. *Slow, slow, slow*

As you will quickly realize, this is not very usable as is on a video stream.

The trick here is actually to turn down the resolution of the input buffer, do the grabcut on that lower-resolution mat, and get the grabcut mask. Then, do the copy using the full-sized picture and the mask retrieve from grabcut on a lower resolution.

This time, we'll create an **in-front** function, which will be a slightly updated version of the preceding, but now including a pyr-down–pyr-up dance around the grabcut call (Figure 4-27).

To make this easier, we'll set the number of iterations of the dance as a parameter of the callback.

```
(defn in-front [resolution-factor buffer]
  (let [
        img (clone buffer)
        rect (new-rect
          (new-point 5 5)
          (new-size (- (.width buffer) 5) (- (.height buffer)
          5 )))
        mask (new-mat)
        pfg-mask (new-mat)
        source1 (new-mat 1 1 CV_8U (new-scalar 3.0))
        pfg_foreground (-> buffer (u/mat-from)  (set-to
        (new-scalar 0 0 0)))]
    (dotimes [_ resolution-factor] (pyr-down! img))
    (grab-cut img mask rect (new-mat) (new-mat) 7 GC_INIT_WITH_RECT)
    (dotimes [_ resolution-factor] (pyr-up! mask))

    (compare mask source1 pfg-mask CMP_EQ)
    (copy-to buffer pfg_foreground pfg-mask)
    pfg_foreground))
```

Then, call simple-cam-window with this new callback.

```
(u/simple-cam-window (partial in-front 2))
```

It's hard to get the feeling of speed by just reading, so do go ahead and try this locally.

Usually, a factor of 2 for the resolution-down dance is enough, but it depends on both your video hardware and the speed of the underlying processor.

Figure 4-27. *As fast as you want, baby*

4-8 Finding an Orange in Real Time
Problem

You would like to detect and track an orange in a video stream. It could also be a lemon, but the author ran out of lemons so we will use an orange.

Solution

Here we will use techniques you have seen before, like **hough-circles** or **find-contours**, and apply them to real-time streaming. We'll draw the shape of the moving orange on the real-time stream.

For either of the solutions, you probably remember that the buffer needs some minor preprocessing to detect the orange. Here, to keep things simple, we'll do a simple **in-range** processing in the hsv color space.

317

How it works

Using Hough-Circles

First, we'll focus on finding the proper hsv range by taking a one-shot picture of the orange.

First, let's put the orange on the table (Figure 4-28).

Figure 4-28. *Orange on the table, Annecy, France*

We first switch to hsv color space, then apply the in-range function, and finally dilate the found orange shape a bit so it's easier for the coming hough-circle call.

In origami, this gives

```
(def hsv (-> img clone (cvt-color! COLOR_RGB2HSV)))
(def thresh-image (new-mat))
(in-range hsv (new-scalar 70 100 100) (new-scalar 103 255 255)
thresh-image)

(dotimes [_ 1]
  (dilate! thresh-image (new-mat)))
```

Now, you'll remember how to do hough-circles from Chapter 3, so no need to spend too much time on that here. The important thing in this part is to have the proper radius range for the orange, and here we take a 10–50 pixels diameter to identify the orange.

```
(def circles (new-mat))
(def minRadius 10)
(def maxRadius 50)
(hough-circles thresh-image circles CV_HOUGH_GRADIENT 1
minRadius 120 15 minRadius maxRadius)
```

At this stage, you should have only one matching circle for the orange. It is quite important to work on this step until exactly one circle is found.

As a check, printing the circle mat should give you a 1×1 mat, like the following:

```
#object[org.opencv.core.Mat 0x3547aa31 Mat [ 1*1*CV_32FC3,
isCont=true, isSubmat=false, nativeObj=0x7ff097ca7460,
dataAddr=0x7ff097c4b980 ]]
```

Once you have the mat nailed, let's draw a pink circle on the original image (Figure 4-29).

```
(def output (clone img))
(dotimes [i (.cols circles)]
  (let [ circle (.get circles 0 i) x (nth circle 0) y (nth
  circle 1) r (nth circle 2)  p (new-point x y)]
  (opencv3.core/circle output p (int r) color/ color/magenta- 3)))
```

Figure 4-29. *Orange and magenta*

Everything is there, so let's wrap up our discoveries as a single function working on the buffer from the video stream; we'll call that function **my-orange!**, which is a recap of the previous steps.

```
(defn my-orange! [img]
  (u/resize-by img 0.5)
  (let [ hsv (-> img clone (cvt-color! COLOR_RGB2HSV))
         thresh-image (new-mat)
         circles (new-mat)
         minRadius 10
         maxRadius 50
         output (clone img)]
(in-range hsv (new-scalar 70 100 100) (new-scalar 103 255 255)
thresh-image)
(dotimes [_ 1]
 (dilate! thresh-image (new-mat)))

(hough-circles thresh-image circles CV_HOUGH_GRADIENT 1
minRadius 120 15 minRadius maxRadius)

(dotimes [i (.cols circles)]
  (let [ circle (.get circles 0 0) x (nth circle 0) y
  (nth circle 1) r (nth circle 2)  p (new-point x y)]
```

```
(opencv3.core/circle output p (int r) color/magenta- 3)))
output))
```

Now it's a simple matter of again passing that callback function to the simple-cam-window.

```
(u/simple-cam-window my-orange!)
```

Figures 4-30 and 4-31 show how the orange is found properly, even in low-light conditions. Winter in the French Alps after a storm did indeed make the evening light, and everything under it, a bit orange.

Figure 4-30. *Orange on a printer*

Figure 4-31. *Mei and oranges*

Using Find-Contours

Instead of looking for a perfect circle, you may be looking for a slightly distorted shape, and this is when using find-contours actually gives better results than hough-circles.

Here we combine the same hsv range found a few minutes ago to select the orange and apply the find-contours technique from Chapter 3.

The **find-my-orange!** callback brings back the familiar find-contours and draw-contours function calls. Note that we draw the contour of found shapes only if those are bigger than the smallest expected size of the orange.

```
(defn find-my-orange! [img ]
 (let[ hsv (-> img clone (cvt-color! COLOR_RGB2HSV))
      thresh-image (new-mat)
      contours (new-arraylist)
      output (clone img)]

 (in-range hsv (new-scalar 70 100 100) (new-scalar 103 255 255)
thresh-image)

 (find-contours
   thresh-image
   contours
   (new-mat)   ; mask
   RETR_LIST
   CHAIN_APPROX_SIMPLE)

 (dotimes [ci (.size contours)]
 (if (> (contour-area (.get contours ci)) 100 )
   (draw-contours output contours ci color/pink-1 FILLED)))
 output))
```

Giving this callback to simple-cam-window shows Mei playing around with a pink-colored orange in Figure 4-32.

Figure 4-32. *Mei and the pink orange, playing at a theater nearby*

4-9 Finding an Image Within the Video Stream

Problem

You would like to find the exact replica of an image within a stream.

Solution

OpenCV comes with feature detection functions that you can use. Unfortunately, those features are mostly Java oriented.

This recipe will show how to bridge Java and Origami, and how using Clojure helps a bit by reducing boilerplate code.

Here we will use three main OpenCV objects:

- FeatureDetector,

- DescriptorExtractor,

- DescriptorMatcher.

Feature extraction works by finding keypoints of both the input picture and the to-be-found image using a feature detector. Then, you compute a descriptor from each of the two sets of points using a descriptor extractor.

Once you have the descriptors, those can be passed as input to a descriptor matcher, which gives a matching result as a set of matches, with each match being given a score via a distance property.

We can then eventually filter points that are the most relevant and draw them on the stream.

The code listings are a bit longer than usual, but let's get this last recipe working on your machine too!

How it works

For this example, we will be looking around for my favorite body soap, eucalyptus scent, both in still images and in real time.

Figure 4-33 shows the concerned body soap.

Figure 4-33. *Petit Marseillais*

Still Image

The first test is to be able to find the body soap in a simple still picture, like the one in Figure 4-34.

Figure 4-34. *Carmen, where in the world is my body soap?*

To get started, we need a few more Java object imports, namely, the detector and the extractor, which we will initialize straightaway before doing any processing.

```
(ns wandering-moss
  (:require
    [opencv3.core :refer :all]
    [opencv3.utils :as u])
  (:import
    [org.opencv.features2d Features2d DescriptorExtractor
    DescriptorMatcher FeatureDetector]))

(def detector (FeatureDetector/create FeatureDetector/AKAZE))
(def extractor  (DescriptorExtractor/create
DescriptorExtractor/AKAZE))
```

Basic setup is done; we then load the body soap background through a short origami pipeline and ask the detector to detect points on it.

```
(def original
  (-> "resources/chapter04/bodysoap_bg.png" imread (u/resize-by
0.3)))
```

```
(def mat1 (clone original))
(def points1 (new-matofkeypoint))
(.detect detector mat1 points1)
```

The coming step is not required whatsoever, but drawing the found keypoints gives an idea of where the matcher thinks the important points are in the mat.

```
(def show-keypoints1 (new-mat))
(Features2d/drawKeypoints mat1 points1 show-keypoints1
(new-scalar 255 0 0) 0)
(u/mat-view show-keypoints1)
```

This gives a bunch of blue circles, as shown in Figure 4-35.

Figure 4-35. *Keypoints of the bodysoap background*

Of course, it may be useful to clean up and remove imperfections before retrieving keypoints, but let's check how the matching works on the raw mat.

Note how the intensity of the points is already pretty strong on the body soap itself.

We now repeat the same steps for a body soap–only mat.

```
(def mat2
  (-> "resources/chapter04/bodysoap.png" imread (u/resize-by 0.3)))

(def points2 (new-matofkeypoint))
(.detect detector mat2 points2)
```

Here again, this drawing points part is not required but it helps to give a better idea of what is going on.

```
(def show-keypoints2 (new-mat))
(Features2d/drawKeypoints mat2 points2 show-keypoints2 (new-
scalar 255 0 0) 0)
(u/mat-view show-keypoints2)
```

The detector result is in Figure 4-36, and again, the keypoints look to be focused on the label of the body soap.

Figure 4-36. *Detector result on the body soap*

The next step is to extract two feature sets that will then be used with the matcher.

This is simply a matter of calling compute on the extractor with the sets of found points from the previous step.

```
(def desc1 (new-mat))
(.compute extractor mat1 points1 desc1)

(def desc2 (new-mat))
(.compute extractor mat2 points2 desc2)
```

Now, on to the matching step. We create a matcher through DescriptorMatcher and give it a way to find out matches.

In IT, brute force is always the recommended way to find a solution. Just try every single solution and see if any match.

```
(def matcher
  (DescriptorMatcher/create DescriptorMatcher/BRUTEFORCE_
  HAMMINGLUT))

(def matches (new-matofdmatch))
(.match matcher desc1 desc2 matches)
```

As was said in the solution summary, each match is rated on how good it is through its **distance** value.

If printed, each match looks something like the following:

```
#object[org.opencv.core.DMatch 0x38dedaa8 "DMatch [queryIdx=0,
trainIdx=82, imgIdx=0, distance=136.0]"]
```

With the distance value, the score of the match itself usually shows up as a value between 0 and 300.

So now, let's create a quick Clojure function to sort and filter good matches. This is simply done by filtering on their distance property. We will filter on matches that are below 50. You may reduce or increase that value as needed, depending on the quality of the recording.

```
(defn best-n-dmatches2[dmatches]
  (new-matofdmatch
    (into-array org.opencv.core.DMatch
      (filter #(< (.-distance %) 50) (.toArray dmatches)))))
```

The **draw-matches** method is a coding nightmare, but it can be seen as mostly a wrapper around the nightmarish drawMatches Java method from the OpenCV.

We mostly pass the parameters the way they are expected using Java interop and some cleanup on each parameter. We also create the output mat bigger, so that we can fit in the background picture and the body soap on the same mat.

```
(defn draw-matches [_mat1 _points1 _mat2 _points2 _matches]
  (let[ output (new-mat
          (* 2 (.rows _mat1))
          (* 2 (.cols _mat1))
          (.type _mat1))
        _sorted-matches (best-n-dmatches2 _matches)]
    (Features2d/drawMatches
            _mat1
            _points1
            _mat2
            _points2
            _sorted-matches
            output
            (new-scalar 255 0 0)
            (new-scalar 0 0 255)
            (new-matofbyte)
            Features2d/NOT_DRAW_SINGLE_POINTS)
    output))
```

And now, with all this, we can draw the matches found by the matcher, using the preceding function.

We pass it the first and second mats, as well as their respective found key points and the set of matches.

```
(u/mat-view
  (draw-matches mat1 points1 mat2 points2 matches))
```

This, surprisingly after all the obscure coding, works very well, as shown in Figure 4-37.

Figure 4-37. *Drawing matches*

Video Stream

Compared to what you have just been through, the video stream version is going to feel like a breath of fresh air.

We will create a **where-is-my-body-soap!** function that will reuse the matcher defined in the preceding and run the detector, extractor, and **match** within the stream callback on the buffer mat.

The previously defined draw-matches function is also reused to draw the matches on the real-time stream.

```
(defn where-is-my-body-soap! [buffer]
  (let[ mat1 (clone buffer)
        points1 (new-matofkeypoint)
        desc1 (new-mat)
        matches (new-matofdmatch)]
    (.detect detector mat1 points1)
    (.compute extractor mat1 points1 desc1)
    (.match matcher desc1 desc2 matches)
    (draw-matches mat1 points1 mat2 points2 matches)))
```

And you can use that callback to simple-cam-window but ... Ah! It seems Mei has found the body soap just before this recipe feature detection could be run!

Figure 4-38 shows both on the video stream.

Figure 4-38. *Thanks for finding the body soap, Mei!*

This brings this recipe, chapter, and book to a humble end. We do hope this gave you plenty of ideas for things to try out by playing with the Origami framework and bringing light to your creation.

For now, "Hello Goodnight":

Searching the sky

I swear I see shadows falling

Could be an illusion

A sound of hidden warning

Fame will forever leave me wanting

Wanting

Well it's alright

I've been alright

Hello Hello Goodnight

Mamas Gun
"Hello Goodnight"

Index

V

Get the eBook for only $5!

Why limit yourself?

With most of our titles available in both PDF and ePUB format, you can access your content wherever and however you wish—on your PC, phone, tablet, or reader.

Since you've purchased this print book, we are happy to offer you the eBook for just $5.

To learn more, go to http://www.apress.com/companion or contact support@apress.com.

Apress®

Printed in the United States
By Bookmasters